Unshakable Faith

Twenty Testimonies by
Men & Women of Great Faith

Tomika Prouty

Printed in the United States of America

ISBN-978-0-578709-1-0-9

House of Stone Publishing
Bonaire - Georgia

Unshakable Faith

Twenty Testimonies by
Men & Women of Great Faith

Tomika Prouty

Table of Contents

This book is dedicated
To The One and True Living God.
To His Son our Lord and Savior Jesus Christ.
To The Precious Holy Spirit.

Walking By Faith

Evangelist Tomika Prouty

"For we walk by faith, not by sight"
2 Corinthians 5:7 KJV

I was born and raised in Macon, Georgia. I grew up in an impoverished neighborhood called Unionville. A city known for its drug dealers who were literally on every corner. It was as if they felt a sense of entitlement, freely encamping themselves in my neighborhood, and around my sanctuary; the place I called home. Growing up in the "hood" wasn't a passport to bad behavior. My mom instilled in us early that we were in the environment, but the environment was not a part of us. My sanctuary included living with my mom, grandparents, great grandmother, three siblings, two uncles, and an aunt.

My mom and maternal elders made sure we knew about Jesus Christ at an early age. We attended Sunday School, Church, Vacation Bible School, Revivals and participated in community marches. I vividly remember marching the streets carrying lighted candles with my church, stopping to plead with the drug dealers to leave the neighborhood and give their lives to God. My inner sanctuary was a single room shared with my siblings and our mom. I am forever grateful for my humble beginnings and early introduction to my Lord and Savior. My mom met the love of her life, Christopher, in 1981. They were married at my childhood church, Center Hill Baptist Church in Macon, Georgia.

I was young when my mom and dad married and often forgot he wasn't my biological father. He treated my sisters and I with a lot of love and respect. He worked for the government, and after they were married, we moved to Texas. The move provided us with a much different lifestyle than the one we experienced in Macon. We instantly went from low-income to middle class. Unfortunately, my mom became homesick, as this was her first time away from her family. Despite the seemingly successful union, the marriage ended in divorce. Shortly after that we returned to Macon and lived in the very same neighborhood in Unionville. My mom did her absolute best to make sure we were safe, clean and properly nurtured. Thank God for our family.

I was the leader among my siblings and assisted my mom with taking care of us. I naturally assumed a certain amount of responsibilities. Not because I had to, or was forced to because my mom did a great job taking care of us. My "take-charge" attitude was present at a very early age. During my senior year of high school, we were told recruiters were coming to administer the Armed Services Vocational Aptitude Battery (ASVAB). I had no desire to join the military at that time. However, God has a way of changing plans, and I signed up to take the test. When graduation approached, I knew I could not remain in Macon. I had to escape! However, I was scared I wouldn't be there for my mom and siblings. Nevertheless, I was excited about the opportunity to support them financially, while also fulfilling my dreams to become someone "great".

One day, after much thought and conversation with my dad, I made the decision to join the Army Reserve. I viewed this as a solid option to experience the best of both worlds. I would still be there for my family while also creating a life of my own. However, I would have to leave my family for a short period of time for training. My cousin helped me to prepare for my journey by braiding my hair in micro braids. This single act of kindness from my beloved cousin meant I had one less thing to worry about. I was ready to start this new chapter of my life. I went to Basic Training at Fort Jackson, South Carolina, in the winter of 1993. Having no idea what to expect upon my arrival, I questioned my decision. Internally asking myself, What did you get yourself into? I remember my Drill Sergeant looking at my hair and screaming. You guessed it, the braids had to go. I only had a matter of hours to do so. My battle buddies came to my rescue; mission accomplished. That was my first real experience with camaraderie and it would set the stage for the rest of my military career. After months of hardcore training and military conditioning, I really wasn't prepared to transition back into the civilian lifestyle. Nor was I prepared to return home and face the challenge being unemployed.

My military training and willingness to step up set me apart from my peers. I was able to quickly secure work at a local restaurant and became a Team Leader in no time. Shortly after settling in, Macon experienced one of the worst flood disasters ever. The flood of 1994 would activate my Reserve unit. We were responsible for providing the citizens with water, as the local water supply wasn't safe to drink. It's one event I'll never forget. The infamous Ocmulgee River overflow was a true indication of the depth of this natural disaster. We were all in disbelief. I had never experienced anything of that magnitude in my life. Homes and businesses were severely damaged. Buildings were destroyed, bridges collapsed, caskets uprooted and floated in plain sight.

When my family members came to retrieve water, their faces exuded pride seeing me in uniform. It brought them great joy to see me serving the citizens of our city. My family could not be prouder of the woman I had become at the tender age of eighteen. After six months, I decided that the Army Reserve and restaurant life was not for me. I needed more of a challenge and an increase in finances. In 1995 I called the recruiter who assisted me with my enlistment in the Army Reserve in 1993 and discussed enlisting in the Active Army. This is where my real journey began! Fast-forward to 2008. We were still at war and my time finally came to answer the call. It was time to trade in the sunny weather of Hawaii for a more rugged terrain and combat gear. Afghanistan, here I come! However, I had to get to Fort Campbell first. Ft. Campbell, Kentucky, home of the 101st Airborne (Screaming Eagles). I was anxious to go to war yet nervous about leaving my family, especially my son. I was going to a place I'd never been, with people I did not know (as I had only been with my new unit about forty-five days) living and working in less than desirable conditions and I did not know what to expect. Although I am a Christian, I quite frankly had thoughts of not returning home.

Despite having faith, I still knew the reality of war. My anxiety started kicking in and I became sad, frustrated and even angry. As I sat in briefings listening to reasons why we must go to war, my anger, sadness and frustration turned to excitement. Yes, I know, weird! I was ready to go to war! Even if I wasn't, I had no choice. As I prepared for war, I was also preparing my military records for the Sergeant First Class (SFC) selection board. My peers told me I would not be selected to SFC on my first look because I did not meet any of the prerequisites. Additionally, the promotion rate on your first look is almost impossible for my Military Occupational Specialty (MOS). My take-charge attitude compelled me to move forward with the paperwork. I submitted it and waited for the results.

Fast-forward, I was selected! Don't tell me what God

can't do and people wonder why I praise Him the way that I do! Training complete. I enlisted in the military to serve, protect and defend our Country. Wheels up! Wheels down! I could not believe I arrived in Afghanistan two days before Christmas. The weather was nice at the location I was assigned to. It reminded me of my assignments in Miami and Hawaii. As we settled in I started becoming anxious, nervous and scared once again. I began to pray and ask God to see us through this deployment and protect us from our enemy. Fast-forward! I returned home from Afghanistan with anxiety, depression and embarrassment. I didn't know how to process or deal with the emotions and the anxiety disorder from my deployment. These issues were further impacted by the emotional and physical trauma my son was subjected to while I was deployed. I was enraged to discover that while I was fighting for our country, my son was fighting for his life. The solution to my trauma was to suppress the issues, and I did for years. Unfortunately, my deployment issues resurfaced. This time there was no way I could pretend everything was ok. I remember having back-to-back anxiety attacks.

They initially started once a week then progressed to a few times a week, then a couple of times a day. I could remember only wanting to feel normal again, the way I felt before Afghanistan. I was exhausted from constantly going to the emergency room for these episodes. I was sick and tired of being sick and tired. One night while my husband was deployed, I started having an anxiety attack. Yes, I was scared but by this time I had enough. I refused to give him (the enemy) my life. I was ready to fight. I laid prostrate on a black rug in my family room (I still own this rug) and cried out to God. I cried, prayed and cried some more, like I had never before.

My husband kept me lifted in prayer even from afar. I knew God wanted to hear my cry, so I cried out! I laid hands on myself and when I got up, my throat was sore, but God had answered my prayers. I was instantly healed. I have not had another anxiety attack since 30 May 2015. Has the enemy tried me? Absolutely, with multiple deaths in my family and constant spiritual warfare. The enemy was mad that God healed me from my anxiety attacks almost five years ago. However, the war began to now wage on depression. The enemy saw how God had positioned me to help veterans and civilians who suffer from anxiety and depression. He knew God would take me places he was incapable and lead me out of depression.

The enemy tried to abort God's plan for my life with altered thinking, but he failed miserably. I know beyond a shadow of a doubt that having a relationship with God kept me from total destruction from the enemy. He may have interfered with God's plan for my life but he did not have the power to abort it. Many people blame God when they go through dark times in their lives. I don't see it that way, because despite it all, God's hands have always been on my life. His praise is always on my lips. *Jeremiah 29:11 KJV, "For I know the thoughts that I think toward you, saith the Lord, thoughts of peace, and not of evil, to give you an expected end."* I had nightmares from deployment, dark vivid dreams would appear and for a time I thought I was going crazy!

The enemy was not going to win! I understand that I had to go through a test in order to have a testimony. I could now effectively minister to others, especially Veterans like me. After years of prayer, I was finally fighting the enemy back with the power of God. I thought I was fighting him before, but in reality, I allowed him to fight me. I was afraid to talk to other Christians as most are judgmental, insensitive and arrogant. Unfortunately, they had forgotten the battles they fought before Christ healed them. I had Christian women tell me, you are not praying hard enough, another asked, is your husband praying for you? The answers were yes and yes. Often our Christian colleagues rationalize their insensitive gestures by immature expression and placing unnecessary blame on you, further pushing you into the pits of depression.

They were correct, however delivery is important in any ministry. *Timothy 1:7 KJV states, "For God hath not given us the spirit of fear; but of power, and of love, and a sound mind."* I knew God's Will was not for me to battle depression indefinitely and that everything happens for a reason. In the end, God will get the Glory. Anxiety and depression was not for me, it was for others. I was chosen to bear the burden in order to witness to the hurt, lost and unsaved effectively. God knew He could trust me to carry out this assignment. He gave me just enough strength to endure and not fail. They say God gives His greatest battles to His strongest warriors. I didn't understand it while walking through the fire, but I now know it was all part of His master plan. Every negative situation will have a positive outcome. Understanding that trials and tribulations produce victory.

Most people want to hear how you went through the fire and came out unscathed. They want to connect with you and know that you understand their pain. We must be obedient to God even in trying seasons. In those seasons, are you seeking the Lord or are you allowing the enemy to defeat you? There's always a lesson to be learned. *Jeremiah 17:7 KJV states, "Blessed is the man that trusteth in the Lord, and whose hope the Lord is."* Despite what it looks like, trust God! You cannot allow the enemy to stop you. Yes, there will be speed bumps, yield signs and even stop signs, keep pressing! God will level the mountains. You will not spend years climbing them. If you follow His instructions, He will equip you to walk over them. *Matthew 17:20 KJV states, "If ye have faith as a grain of mustard seed, ye shall say unto this mountain, Remove hence to yonder place; and it shall remove; and nothing shall be impossible unto you."* I have been chosen to help those who suffer with anxiety, depression and suicidal thoughts because of the lack of sensitivity in the world and especially in the Church. Somewhere in my season (battling anxiety and depression), I began to feel inadequate. I felt misunderstood and I always wondered why I never fit in.

The enemy began to fill my mind with lies. I had to take every thought captive and combat his lies with the truth of God's Word. Years passed and I began to form a more intimate relationship with God and He began to heal me. I no longer felt the need for validation by others. I don't mind being unique, I don't mind not fitting in and I certainly don't feed into the spirit of inadequacy. Through fervent prayer, meditation, reading the Word, Praise and Worship, journaling, and yes, even exercising, God began to move mightily in my life. I walk by faith NOT by sight!

MEET EVANGELIST TOMIKA PROUTY

Evangelist Tomika Prouty is the Co-Founder of Truth Revealed Global Ministries (Street/Outreach). She enjoys serving others. Her areas of expertise include leadership, mentorship and training. She served 22 years in the United States Army (Retired) and is a Combat Veteran with one tour in Afghanistan. Evangelist Tomika enjoys spending time with her family, furthering her education, reading and writing for various organizations, while also expanding her company, House of Stone by CoCo, LLC and more!

Connect with Evangelist Tomika Prouty:

Instagram: @StrengthDespiteAdversity
@HouseOfStoneByCoCo
Website: www.TomikaProuty.com

www.facebook.com/HouseofStonebyCoCo

Prodigal Son

Pastor Craig Prouty

It all started before my birth. While I was in my mother's womb, she and her best friend, Sheryl, prayed that I would be a strong man of God. She eventually gave birth on December 3, 1977.

I remember growing up feeling like I was robbed of a normal life. I felt that other people had it easier as they always seemed happy. My mother would often ask me why are you angry? I never told her why. However, I always thought to myself, you would be angry too if your parents divorced while you were in kindergarten. My parents' divorce led to my siblings and I being displaced. This displacement led us on a journey through a few foster homes.

I always felt like I was different from other kids my age. Growing up in Spring Lake Park, Minnesota, I would always look up to the picture of Jesus and ask why He would allow my family to separate like this. I later discovered that God allows all of us to do whatever we want, hoping we would one day choose Him. I remember one day before school watching the "700 Club," and it finally happened, I accepted Jesus Christ as my Lord and Savior. I didn't know the magnitude of my actions but I didn't want to miss an opportunity to have peace in a chaotic life.

I remembered moving back home with my mother and I was elated. Yet I still felt hurt and anger for the lost time. I would take all that unsettled energy and put it into sports rather than a relationship with God. That never stopped my mother from attempting to have my sisters, brothers and I in church almost every Sunday. She would continue to pray over us, desiring that we would one day live our lives wholeheartedly for Christ.

In my past I rarely chose the right people to hang with, and by doing so, I stayed grounded or in trouble. I always thought that rules only applied to other folks and not me. I backed that up by judging others based on their actions, while judging myself solely on my intentions. This helped me to stay angry. I continually felt as if I always got the raw end of the deal, not realizing the sacrifices of my mother and stepfather. If I had forgiven them, I would have been able to release the anger inside and break free from the grip I was allowing the devil to have on me. Not yet realizing that God's love could conquer any and all of my sins.

During my high school years, I bounced back and forth from my mom to my dad's home. My dad finally became fed up with me bouncing back and forth, giving me an ultimatum. He told me that if I moved back to my mom's that I couldn't move back to his place. That worked out well until one day, I got into an argument with my mother about some car insurance. I left taking my uninsured self to my girlfriend uncle's house. I quickly had to support myself, because I was never returning home. I remember sitting in class thinking to myself about the ways in which I was earning money to support myself. These methods for survival would either get me killed or put into jail.

So, I decided to join the Army Reserve. I thought that going full time in the military might not be a good idea because I had a mouth on me as well as an attitude problem. I figured if I liked the Army Reserve, then maybe one day I could go active duty. So, there I was 16 years old having to ask my mom for permission to join the military. I figured this Army thing would be my ticket out of the life I was living. I soon became tired of the Reserve and wanted to go active duty. After jumping through some hoops, I finally got an active duty assignment. The weekend before leaving for my first duty assignment, I was placed in jail because of an argument with my sister while she was pregnant. She refused to get out of my way, so I picked her up and physically moved her out the way. I wanted to hang with some friends and get drunk (no, I did not hit her, but touching her without permission was enough to land me in jail). Forgetting something back at the house caused me to return. Upon entering the driveway, I was greeted by Ramsey County's finest. Once again, not taking any responsibility for my actions, I built resentment towards my sisters for calling the police. Not realizing this was a blessing in disguise, as I probably would have done something stupid or possibly got a DUI.

Here I was on active duty, finally thinking I could live my life any way I pleased. The only problem with that mindset is that it often got me in trouble. I figured that if I worked hard, I could play hard. Playing hard was what I did. I lifted weights, played softball and partied with no consequences (or at least I thought). There would be times early in my military career where I would attend church, and the Pastor, Preacher, Apostle and or Bishop would come up to me and tell me I was supposed to stop running from God! They said that one day I was to become a Preacher. They would also tell me I would be a great leader for Christ one day. That was typically when I became nervous and scared, thinking to myself, "how could God forgive me for all the wrongs I had done?" I was miserable, missing my daughter. I contacted her mom to propose marriage, in an effort to have my daughter with me. I resented my biological father for not being around and I did not want my daughter to have the same resentment towards me. We eventually got married but never grasped the concept of what marriage meant to God. I continued to play softball and lift weights and wonder why my wife would always complain about feeling alone. We eventually divorced. My drinking finally got the best of me as I was kicked off the softball team. I later got a D.U.I and was forced to go to the military rehab program.

Now remarried. I stayed sober for about two and a

half years until my wife wanted to have a drink with me. At that time, I remember reminding her that she came to pick me up from rehab with my supervisor. I know that it was still my choice to take the drink, and by no means am I blaming her. That night started an eight-year drink-a-thon. We eventually divorced.

I finally put the plug in the jug after the second divorce. I asked God to deliver me from my alcoholic state of mind and I also asked God to help me to be the man He designed me to be. I thanked God for restoration and for His grace and mercy. I remember attending Saturday morning intercessory prayer with my deacon and him leaning over to whisper that I would find my wife at my next duty assignment. I was skeptical. I then asked God to help me be the husband he wanted me to be.

I flew into Honolulu, Hawai'i, where I was greeted by Tomika, who is now my wife and her son is now our son. She showed me around the Island, and we hit it off well. I loved that we both put God first and attended church whenever the doors were open. The Chaplain at the time asked if I would be interested in helping around the Church. I told him I would love to help any way I could and I started that Sunday. This action initiated my first assignment as an Usher and later turned into leading Wednesday night Bible Study. I loved preparing the lesson, doing research, and just spending time with God. I loved that I was gaining wisdom and strengthening my relationship with God. We later moved to Georgia (Ft. Stewart), continuing our military career.

I didn't realize it at the time, but God was preparing us to birth a ministry. God had one Pastor ordain me as a minister, and a Bishop ordained me as an Elder. Thus, installing me as a Pastor to our ministry "New Beginnings International Outreach Ministries" Now known as "Truth Revealed Global Ministries." God has not only birthed a ministry through my Queen and I, but He has also allowed both of us to publish several books and also create a Daily Devotional App "Daily Message Truth Revealed". The daily devotional came to life through the passing of my father from stage four cancer. I remember praying to God about how I could help my family cope while at the hospital during his last days. God told me that since I spend so much time in His Word I should write down what it means and share the message with people He would put on my heart. He also showed me that I was to pray for those folks that I sent the devotional to. I am eternally grateful for who God has allowed me to become, as I am nothing without Him. To God Be The Glory!

MEET PASTOR CRAIG PROUTY

Pastor Craig A. Prouty is the Founder of Truth Revealed Global Ministries (Street/Outreach). His areas of expertise include leadership, mentorship and training. He enjoys serving others not being served. He dedicated

23 years in the United States Army (Retired) (including time served in the Army Reserve) and is a Combat Veteran with one tour in Afghanistan, two tours in Iraq and numerous missions around the Globe. When not hard at work, Pastor Craig enjoys spending time with his family and golfing.

Connect with Pastor Craig Prouty:

Truth Revealed Global Ministries App (**available for download**).

Factory Reset...The Second Chance God

Natasha Sumter

Quest for love. Young adults often think they know what "love" is. Dictionaries define it for us, movies and T.V. shows fantasize it through "love stories", preachers teach about it, some people emulate love with public displays of affection and compromising with their loved ones. Is that the unconditional love God wants us to experience? Do we know what love is? Do we understand what love means, what it looks like or how it should feel?

I grew up in Lower Alabama, or "LA." I thought I understood what "love" was. I had fallen in and out of "like-love" and just wanted "real love." I suffered a couple heartbreaks and stepped away from relationships for a while. I was an Army Reservist assigned to Detachment 1, 191st Maintenance Company, in Dothan, Alabama. I was accepted into Tuskegee University's Veterinary Program, so I began chatting with my Unit's Administrator about my educational benefits. One day, a guy I thought was extra SUPER cute was in the office talking to her. She introduced us and we hit it off. Our conversation seemed to flow. He lived in Georgia, maybe an hour away from where I lived. His full-time job made it difficult for us to see each other, so we saw each other during drill. I really liked this guy and he seemed to really like me.

John 10:10 NKJV - The thief does not come except to

steal, and to kill, and to destroy...

The foot hole. During the next few monthly drills, we hung out and got to know each other better. The door to my heart was ajar and our relationship evolved. I trusted him and we became closer and we eventually became intimate. I mean, we were both single…right? During one of the very few encounters, I got pregnant. I was afraid and nervous to talk with him about the pregnancy. I was 19 years old, working at the Ft. Rucker Exchange and living with my parents. Pregnant, I was on a journey of uncertainty and needed to know that he would be there for us. Born and raised in the church, I felt shame, guilt, and that I had disappointed God. Although he was older and we both knew better, I only blamed myself for the pregnancy. As a "Christian," I knew better than to lay down with a man who wasn't my husband.

Lost faith. I nervously pulled up my "big girl draws" and called him. I told him I needed to talk with him about something very important. He agreed to meet me near our Reserve Unit. I didn't know what to expect but I hoped for the best. Instead, the news was met with the crushing response, "What are you going to do?" I was paralyzed and overwhelmed with a flood of emotions – hurt, fear, anger, guilt, shame, desperation, sadness, grief, etc. I no longer knew what I was going to do and questioned if I even knew the right answer. For the first time I contemplated an abortion.

II Corinthians 10:4-6 NKJV - For the weapons of our warfare are not carnal but mighty in God for pulling down strongholds, casting down arguments and every high thing that exalts itself against the knowledge of God, bringing every thought into captivity to the obedience of Christ, and being ready to punish all disobedience when your obedience is fulfilled.

Now what?! I told my mom about the pregnancy. Feeling alone and engrossed with emotions, I was against the clock and had to make a decision. I found out that while I was pregnant, he had a girlfriend who was also pregnant. I thought, "I have to do this!" I made the hardest decision in my life – to have an abortion. That night I cried myself to sleep as I replayed the conversations in my mind. The flood of emotions quickly became a tsunami that tossed me "to and fro" like a ragdoll. I no longer knew who I was or Whose I was. The tears only seemed to stop long enough for me to fall asleep; however, continued to flow even as I slept. My damning moment was when I woke up the next morning, knowing my total income wouldn't be enough to support me and my baby – pay for formula, daycare, utilities, rent an apartment (where I felt safe), buy a car and get insurance, etc. I knew what I had to do, but I didn't want to do it. My faith was taking a beating and I wasn't strong enough to do anything other than the inevitable.

This is my truth. In July 1991, I made that dreaded appointment to abort my beautiful baby. Before I walked my "Green Mile", I met a nice (older) Soldier. I was honest with him about my situation. He became my best and only friend at that time. There was no way I could tell anyone else about what I was going through. I knew I would be judged even more, so I relied on his friendship to get me through. He knew what was about to happen and still chose to stand by my side. A few weeks later, it was done…finished. Knowing what I had done made me feel empty and the bright smile that once earned me the nickname "Smiley" from my Bishop, struggled to surface. I pretended to be OK and quickly mastered the skill of internalizing my truth. I didn't want anyone to know that "Smiley" had sinned and even worse, had an abortion. My guilt condemned me! My shame mocked me! The devil had my mind and told me I couldn't talk to God about anything anymore. I thought God had stopped loving me and stopped hearing me. There was an eerie silence in my life, not because God wasn't there, but because I didn't feel worthy of Him, His love, His presence or His forgiveness. I turned my back on God so I wouldn't sense His sadness and He wouldn't see mine…humph, as if! I was convinced that if I stopped going to church God wouldn't see me or my shame. I felt like a woman without a face. An unclean spirit had attached itself and infected me with untruths. I was in warfare and had no idea how to stop the voices and thoughts in my head.

Ephesians 4:20-23 NKJV - But you have not so

learned Christ, if indeed you have heard Him and have been taught by Him, as the truth is in Jesus: that you put off, concerning your former conduct, the old man which grows corrupt according to the deceitful lusts, and be renewed in the spirit of your mind, and that you put on the new man which was created according to God, in true righteousness and holiness.

Finding God again. Several months later, I married the gent that was with me through my truth. I couldn't do that Reserve thingy anymore. I was over it and so much more! I tried to run away by going Active Duty Army. Two years later, I became pregnant with our first child. I was soon stationed in Panama, far away from everything and everyone. There, I found a new identity and began attending the Chapel on Post. I was new and no one knew me except my husband and my Sponsor, but I somehow still felt judged. I attended Bible Study and bonded with some of the Mothers and Sisters in the church. They reintroduced me to God's love, grace and forgiveness. I only had to say yes to Him and allow Him to heal my brokenness. I needed my faith strengthened, a fresh anointing, and a fresh touch of God's hand. I needed to be washed by the Word of God and the Blood of Jesus so I could be cleansed of my sins and freed from the emotions that imprisoned me. I needed a "hard reset."

Ephesians 6:10-13 NKJV - Finally, my brethren, be strong in the Lord and in the power of His might. Put on the whole armor of God that you may be able to stand against the wiles of the devil. For we do not wrestle against flesh and blood, but against principalities, against powers, against the rulers of the darkness of this age, against spiritual hosts of wickedness in the heavenly places. Therefore, take up the whole armor of God that you may be able to withstand in the evil day, and having done all, to stand.

The infection! Think of your total being – your mind, body, and spirit – as a computer network and think of viruses and spyware (or electronic infections) as unclean and familiar spirits. The network is your spirit, the firewall is the armor of God, while the computer is your mind (the data files in the computer are your emotions), your body is represented as the End User and the "Help Desk" are the Holy Spirit, Jesus Christ and God our Heavenly Father. Each member of the Help Desk performs specific roles to resolve issues. In the natural, when our computer becomes infected with a virus or isn't "acting right," we troubleshoot the device before calling the Help Desk. We call the Help Desk when we can't fix it. The Team assesses the system, sees the issue, cleanses the system and applies the necessary security patch(es) in the firewall and asks you to restart your system. However, sometimes the issue is so significant that removing the virus or spyware isn't enough. The device gets quarantined and needs a factory reset to restore it to its original settings – free of third-party programming.

1 John 1:7 NKJV - But if we walk in the light as He is in the light, we have fellowship with one another, and the blood of Jesus Christ His Son cleanses us from all sin.

The problem! Unclean spirits are always awaiting an opportunity to cause us to sin. Like computer viruses, the End User downloads an infected file through a hole in the firewall. The virus attaches itself to the data files in the host; unclean spirits do the same thing. They attach themselves to our ideology of Christianity and what we ***think*** it should look like, versus what it **should be** – obedient, loving, humble, kind, patient, faithful, joyful, thankful, prayerful, praiseful and worshipful of God. Although I was saved, went to church regularly, sang in the choir, helped in the church, gave tithes and offerings (according to my understanding), I lacked a true relationship with Christ but didn't know it. My armor was flawed. I wasn't prepared for the spiritual warfare inflicted by the unclean spirit(s) and the like. Like a computer virus, the unclean spirit attacked my mind. I wasn't filled with the Holy Spirit, so my temple was empty and displayed a "vacancy" sign, welcoming the unclean spirits. After I received the baptism of the Holy Spirit, He evicted the unclean spirits without notice. They were commanded to come out in the name of Jesus!

Second chance God. After God renewed my faith and made me whole again, life was good, so I thought. Seven years and three children later my husband and I divorced. I returned to the "single life." Look, it's easy being saved and married with a husband available to me. However, when I got divorced and became single again, I had to live a **Christian**-single life, dying to the flesh every minute of the day! Go ahead and turn to your (invisible) neighbor and say, "Tash is tell'n the truth!" And if you're bold enough, turn to an actual person and tell them. Take your time, I have popcorn because this is going to get good! They'll either ask you what you are talking about or pull out their can of mace, shake it, and give you the side eye. It isn't easy being saved and single especially after being married and knowing your spouse in a Biblical sense.

Eight years after my husband and I divorced I got pregnant with my fourth child. Matthew 12:43-45 says that when an unclean spirit leaves a host, it travels the world looking for a new home. When it can't find one, it returns to the home it left. Finding the home swept clean, it seeks to take up residency and brings seven other spirits with it, making the home worse than it was before it left the first time. My point? The devil showed up right on queue to remind me of my past. I time traveled back to 1991. This time I was divorced with small children. I sat on my kitchen floor and cried out to the Lord for help. I told God there was no way I could do any of this on my own. I was contrite and broken. I repented and pleaded to God that I needed Him more than ever. I was tired and worn out when the devil reminded me of all the reasons I didn't need another child. But as Jesus Christ is the risen

Son of God, I showed up to the arena with the Holy Spirit. I was prepared for warfare this time! God reminded me of who I was and Whose I was. Yes, I fell, but God's grace empowered me and I rebuked the devourer and reclaimed my baby's life and my salvation through the cleansing Blood of Jesus Christ. God fortified my armor with the baptism and the anointing of the Holy Spirit and I declared the victory. I underwent a "factory reset!" I stopped crying and stood up. I wiped my tears and took a stance. I knew the battle rhythm! The devil wanted my daughter's soul but he couldn't and can't have her. She belongs to God.

The devourer wanted me to abort my child and even tried to kill this testimony. But God said, **ENOUGH!** Someone needs to know that God **is** a forgiving God and that His grace truly is sufficient - II Cor. 12:7-10. I was redeemed by the Holy One because I chose Him and not my flesh. I wanted to please Him. I wanted to be acceptable to Him - Rom. 12:1-2. I couldn't change the past but I knew I could reshape my future through my obedience to God - Duet. 5:33. My beautiful baby girl came into this world with a cry unto the Lord. And for the next two years of her life seemed to never stop crying. My God! We still tease her about how she would cry **us** to sleep. Believe me when I say this, the devil tried to kill her before she took her first breath and some seventeen years later, still hasn't stopped trying.

I Peter 5:8 NKJV - Be sober, be vigilant; because your adversary the devil walks about like a roaring lion, seeking whom he may devour.

MEET NATASHA SUMTER

Ms. Natasha Sumter is a Policy Analyst at the U.S. Department of Energy and Founder and CEO of Natasha Sumter Enterprises, LLC. Her areas of expertise include policy analysis and technical writing; personal and professional coaching, mentoring, and leadership; organizational culture; and strategic planning. She has over 30 years of Military, Federal Government, and Contractor service in Security Administration. Natasha enjoys serving God and her community, singing, ministering, teaching children's church, developing hair care products, editing written works and spending time with her loved ones. "That which we once left behind, will shape the future of our legacy." – Natasha Sumter

Connect with Natasha Sumter:

Email: XceednglyBlessed@gmail.com

Phone: 855-564-6866

Web: www.XceednglyBlessed.com

Twitter: @NatzLyric

Facebook, Instagram & YouTube: XceednglyBlessed

Positioned For Promotion

Teriece Cherell

Have you ever been passed up for a promotion that you felt you deserved? Have you ever felt like you were overlooked for something you wanted? Have you ever worked hard and felt like it was not appreciated? Have you ever felt like you put your all into something or someone and got nothing in return? When I first decided that I wanted to be a part of this collaboration project, I was not initially sure of what I wanted to write. I thought of all the possible testimonies that I could give to encourage others to activate their faith in God and themselves. Of these testimonies, this is the one that stood out most in my mind. Nothing ever happens by chance. Everything happens for a reason and has its time. The only time that we can actively engage in is the present. The past is no longer and the future does not exist yet. Life sometimes takes you on the most indirect paths to get you where you are meant to be. I was laid off from a job that I liked. My position was the Executive Assistant to the Executive Director. I learned my new position fast and well, garnered the admiration of the tenants and implemented some new programs and systems. During my tenure there, I was instrumental in fostering better relationships with the tenants through the use of effective communication and collaboration within the center. Almost a year into the position, they laid me off with no warning. I went to work as usual and prepared for my day.

Two of the board members came into the office and asked to speak with me. I was informed that my services were no longer needed and they were moving in another direction. I was upset, as I did not see it coming and took my job seriously. I was there early, stayed late and would even go on weekends with no pay. However, they provided me with a generous severance package that paid me for the next 3 months. This blessing afforded a little free time before I actively sought employment again. I had two weeks to rest, spend time with my daughter and then began looking for another job. Looking back, I realize the mistake that I made. I sought another job instead of a career. I worked with Corporate Connection Recruiting and Staffing on various assignments until I was placed with my current employer, Republic Business Credit LLC. During the interview process I asked about any future opportunities for growth and advancement. It is always a question that I ask, as I seek frequent opportunities for both personal and professional development. It was in a different industry than I previously worked before.

I began this new journey in October 2016. I was eager and ready to learn about my new position. I am a fast learner and my superiors were pleased with my progress, work ethic and character. I learned in weeks what it had taken other employees months to learn. I asked questions, took notes and sought to be a step ahead. I put my best foot forward, avoided distractions, messy coworkers and made sure always to do more than what was asked or expected of me. I believe that no job description is all-inclusive.

There may be some things not listed that I may be expected to do. You see, my motto is stay ready, so you don't have to get ready. About six months later, another position became available for which I was interested. I had already prepared for this new position by asking questions from colleagues in this position, speaking to my superiors and taking the initiative to try new things. A wise woman told me, "Work the job you want, not the job you have." I reviewed the accounts, researched the companies and remembered those encouraging words that made me smile. Those words would prove to work in my favor sooner than I thought. I remember that one of the sermons during this time was Dates Determine Destiny. I recall that message and began putting the dates in perspective. The position became available in late April of 2017. In biblical numerology, I recall that 5 is the number of favor and grace. The interview was on Friday, May 5, which for me, equated to double favor and grace. God would give me a double dose of favor in my life. Of the other applicants, I felt that I was the most ready and qualified for the task. Still, it was about 2-3 weeks before I heard anything. You know the old folks say, no news is good news. Therefore, I did not want to appear too eager to know who had the position, especially if it was not me. During this time, I prayed, praised, prepared and positioned myself for the promotion that would come. Depending on the nature of the job, it usually takes at least one year before you are eligible to apply for another position. However, as positions and opportunities become available, the company seeks to promote from within before looking outside of the company.

I continued to do my current job to the best of my ability until I learned who had received the promotion. I had faith that God would reward my faithfulness, as He knew what I had been through lately. I was faithful, consistent and never changed who I was. Furthermore, about three weeks after the interview, I was called into the office. I received the promotion and was getting my first salary increase. I was so happy and excited that I wanted to run out of the office screaming and thanking God. I maintained my composure as I walked back to my desk. I contained my screams and shouting until I went to the bathroom. Tears of joy, gratitude and accomplishment ran down my face. This was the first promotion I had received in so short a time. It made me feel good as I frequently say, that sometimes people see things in you that you do not or cannot always see in yourself. You see, this time, I trusted God wholeheartedly and completely. It was going to be His will and His way and there was nothing that anybody could do to stop what God planned. I knew from previous experience that even when the odds were stacked against me, it would work out in my favor. God had done it numerous times before and I knew that He would do it again. A few years earlier, I was in the same situation when my job ended. The company that I worked for had laid us off due to a lack of funding for the program. The program was being phased out and they were laying us off in tiers. I was devastated, as I didn't have a clue of what I would do. I had bills just like the rest of my coworkers, but somehow, I knew that everything was going to be alright. I thought about some of my other coworkers who had children and were single parents. At that time, it was only my dog and I. I was in somewhat of a better situation than them. I was able to get the maximum unemployment allowed, which was about $255.00 at the time.

While this helped me greatly, the issue was that I needed three checks to take care of my monthly expenses, rent, the electricity and phone bill. This did not include money for food, gas and other household things. Yet, even while living paycheck to paycheck, I had shelter, food, water and lights. I had the necessities, which was all I needed. I was grateful that I was not homeless or hungry. Thank God that I also had some help from some willing family members. So, when I found myself in this same situation, I was somewhat disappointed, but I knew that everything would be alright. I knew because I had great faith in God. I believed that He would show how merciful and mighty He was. God sometimes places us in situations or positions that we don't always understand. I know that sometimes even us Christians struggle with trusting God. If we are honest with ourselves, how many times have we tried to comfort someone who has lost a loved one? We all know the old clichés. Trust in the Lord and He will take care of you, lean on His arm, stand on His Word, time heals all wounds and weeping may endure for a night, but joy comes in the morning. We all know the right words to say and scriptures to quote, but how many of us get stressed out, burned out and just want to give up? We pray but do we truly and fully submit to God? Do we wait on Him or do we try to take matters into our own hands? Do we move when it suits us? I was guilty of doing these things. I would say that I trust God, but I would attempt to give Him a hand in what I felt was supposed to happen. Trusting in the Lord is not a phrase. It is an action. It requires us to do something. When we trust God, we give it to Him and move on to something else. We don't worry, complain or fret over it. Fear and faith cannot abide in the same space. We're either going to trust God and let Him do what He does best or we're going to interfere and mess it up. I recall another sermon, which addressed us helping God out and trying to do His job.

I laughed at how many times I "assisted God" in my

life. How I thought I was helping Him move faster but I was doing more harm than good in the situation. When we truly submit to God, we acknowledge His presence and position in our lives. We know that there will be ups and downs, the good and the not so good things in life, but we embrace them for the lessons and blessings that they teach us. As simple as this may sound, it's a hard thing to do. We like to be in control and if we can't control what's happening in our lives, we become frustrated, envious and even agitated; not only with ourselves or others, but even with God.

We must focus on what God has called us to do. We can't control what happens in our lives, but we can control how we respond to it. No matter if times are easy or hard, we can count on God because He is our strength and He can do all things but fail. We all experience things in life that cause us to doubt ourselves, and even God, but the fact is that we are still here, still standing. We could've been blind, crippled or crazy, but God loves us despite our faults, flaws and failures. He favors us and gives His grace and mercy. We never have to question God's loyalty or faithfulness to us because He never changes. He is the same God, yesterday, today and forevermore. If we allow God's love, grace, wisdom and strength to fill us, we will never feel alone, unloved or empty inside. Even though we cannot understand what's going on, we can trust God and know that "All things work together for the good of those who love God and are called according to His purpose". I have learned that God will remove people and things out of your way to make room for you. God does not always call the qualified He qualifies the called. If He places the vision inside of you, He will provide the provisions for you to carry out the tasks. I am a living witness that if your heart is right and you are in alignment with God, things will fall into place. It may not come when you think it should or want it to come. It may not be in the package that is expected or desired, but it comes right on time. When we place God first, our desires will align with His desires for our lives. When we chase after God and righteous living instead of worldly things, we begin to see things more clearly. God gives us clear vision when we are ready and willing to embrace it.

Things began to happen suddenly, immediately, just like that. Doors will open to us and opportunities will arise that we didn't know were possible. I prayed, praised, prepared and because of God's faithfulness to me, I was positioned for the promotion. This was the first promotion of many that I would receive with this company. Little did I know, I would be considered for another promotion six months later. This time, the salary increase came before the official title change. I was not overlooked or looked over for this promotion. I was right where I was meant to be. Life is a test, and as much as we want to pass, we will sometimes fail with flying colors. But that is all right because we serve a forgiving, merciful and mighty God who does not hold grudges. He allows us chance after chance to get it right. If we pray, ask for forgiveness, and sincerely attempt to do better and get better in our lives. Each time He places something in us, look at it as His way of preparing and positioning us for promotion in our lives.

MEET TERIECE CHERELL

Teriece Cherell is a New Orleans native. She is a strong lover of reading, writing, speaking and acting. A romantic at heart, she enjoys walks in the park, spending quality time with her family, traveling to new places, shopping and watching Lifetime movies. When she isn't reading, writing or speaking at various events, she is volunteering for community service projects and sharing her time and talents with young girls and women. Her favorite fashion accessories are sunglasses of all colors, shades and styles.

Connect with Teriece Cherell:

Facebook: www.facebook.com/TeriеceCherell

Instagram: @iamteriececherell

Website: www.teriececherell.com

Don't Bite The Bait

Sandra Earven

At age 12, I began using my body to get money. I chose my pimps out of bars at the tender age of 14. That took me to Jacksonville, Florida, where I began selling my body. I became hooked on drugs and alcohol. One night I met a trick (a man who buys sex) who held me at gunpoint, blindfolded me, put me in the trunk of a car, broke in a house, and raped me. I lived in Atlanta from 16 to 22 years old. One night I took a trick to my house. When I came back to turn the money in, I forgot to give my pimp the keys to the house. Resulting in him saying, "I am going to teach you how to think." He called me an ugly name and beat me for two hours off and on with a police billy stick.

I began working on Stewart Avenue in Atlanta. Another girl and I caught two tricks and took them into our motel room. We didn't know that they had a 45 automatic and were robbers. My pimp came over to the room and knocked on the door because I had stayed there too long. When he opened the door, one guy was standing behind the door. They said that they were going to take me with them because I was a smart "B." My pimp begged them not to take me. He said that he would give them all of the money in his pocket. Once he did that, he thought they would leave. Instead, all three of us lay on the bed face down, and they shot one round into the floor. It could have been in our heads.

My pimp told me to pack everything because we were moving. We went downtown and got another room. As I was unpacking, I realized that I forgot a pair of his snake-skinned shoes. He reached over, got the standing ashtray, and hit me in the mouth. My mouth looked like three lips in one. He wouldn't take me to the emergency room. Instead, he poured Hennessy on my lips for them to heal. Oh! I was in so much pain. He kept me locked in for about two weeks. When the opportunity came for him to put me back on the street, I ran away and came back home to Savannah. When I got to Savannah, I met a trick who took me to the Alamo Plaza on Bay Street on the 12th of May 1984. He stabbed me, beat me in the head with an iron, and choked me with the cord.

As I was dying, I heard angels telling me, "It's alright." I dropped my arms. I guess he thought I was dead. He bear-hugged me and put me in the bathroom, sat me up against the wall, turned on the hot shower, and closed the door. The angels came again as I was trying to turn off the hot water. They told me to come out that it was alright. I got to the phone and told the lady that I had been stabbed. I was stabbed 23 times and left for dead. I lay in the doorway until help arrived. When I was well, I learned that a funeral home came to the Alamo, along with the EMS. I was put in a body bag because they thought I was dead. As they were zipping me up, life came back into my body. In the ambulance, I looked up at the paramedics. I said, "Please don't let me die." I was in a coma for the next five days.

When my mother and brother came to the hospital that night, they were told that they couldn't see me because they had never seen a person cut the way that I had been. They told them to go back home. They would call if I made it. My brother and I never met our father. I never wanted to lie down with my father, so I began asking men their names. Each time I met a client, I asked their name. One client asked, "Do you want my money, or do you want my name?" I stopped asking men their names, but I continued selling my body. After I was well, I went to Miami with a pimp from Savannah. When we got to Florida, he told me that crack was selling faster than my body. I told him, "Give me those two suitcases," and I went about my business. I didn't know, but he was a married man. I lived in Miami for one year and became a stripper. I fell deeper into my sins. I started smoking "wooly" joints in Miami. They are $11 joints already rolled with both crack and reefer.

I missed my mother, and I tried to reach her, but couldn't. I walked the streets of Miami, crying, praying, and talking to the Lord. My mother's phone number changed, and I lost contact with her. I told the Lord that if He helped me get back to Savannah, Georgia, I would make amends with my mother. Sometimes when a child goes astray, the parents feel like it's their fault. I asked my mom to forgive me for living that way because it had been my choice. Yet, I continued to live a destructive lifestyle. I remember wanting to commit suicide because of things coming up in my relationships that I could not understand.

Through it all, God still kept me for such a time as this. In 1995, I was living on 35th Street, as a street harlot. One day I left my keys inside a trick's car, while I went to use the telephone booth to call my rent man. I saw a police car, and I remember thinking, "He's looking for somebody." I had been running from the police for over a year. As I was on the phone, the cop turned around and came back. He said, "Ms. Mack, hang up the phone." I had not reached my rent man but was talking to my mother. I told her that the policeman told me to hang up. She said, "Hang up and go with them," as if she was going to get me out of jail, not so. The officer told me that he had just picked up warrants from the precinct.

That night lead to 11 months in jail. One time, I felt like I had a key to the jailhouse because of the way I was living. In jail, I started reading the Bible and drawing closer to Him. I started praying for a husband. I thought that not having a companion was a big part of my constant backsliding. When I left jail in 1996, I still had the mind to serve Jesus. I went straight to a local Spiritual House because I wanted to remain under the anointing. In the house, there were three other ladies. I continued to serve God, but one day I noticed how the other ladies were living. One was dating another woman;

the others were cursing and talking that same old street talk laced with profanity and vulgar sexual content. I found myself murmuring and complaining. I had taken my eyes off of the Lord. I said to myself, "I don't have to live in this house with them living like that. I can go to hell by myself." I stayed there for about a month and a half; then I remembered a man with a rooming house on 35th Street. I got a room there, where drugs, prostitution, and liquor were an all day, everyday affair. I thought I was ahead of the game because I paid for my rent with my body. I didn't know that my enemy, the devil, had set a trap for me. I started drinking again.

I remember going down to Barnard and 31st Street, where there was a liquor house. I was inside drinking when a friend came in and told me that a man wanted me outside. Once outside, the man said, "Sandra, I came to tell you that you are going to be my wife. Come go to my mama's house with me. I want to propose to you." I didn't go. I asked him when he would get his next pass because he was in the halfway house. He said in two weeks. In two weeks, he came back, took me to his mother's house, and proposed to me. I married him. I had not asked him why he was in a halfway house. Remember, I had prayed for a husband when I was incarcerated, but I left the anointing of the Lord.

The enemy sent me a man. Since I was back in the world, I did not ask God if this man was from him. Why am I saying this? I ended up marrying an unsaved man because I lost my way spiritually. This man turned my whole life upside down. He was abusive physically, emotionally, spiritually, and psychologically. The enemy knows how to dress things up. When you pray for something, always go back - I say again - always go back and ask the Lord whether it was from Him. Satan can send you a substitute. It took several years before I got out of that abusive marriage. I ended up living with another man while I was separated. I tried to commit suicide. At one point, I was lying in the middle of Martin Luther King Boulevard and 38th Street until someone called the police and EMS. I ended up in a mental hospital for psychological evaluation until the doctor came to see me. I told the doctor that I believed the guy I was living with was a trigger. Meaning, that he made me angry and that provoked me to do crazy things. They recommended substance abuse classes for me. I never made it there.

A week later, my cousin and I walked to a package shop. I had been drinking all morning. There was an older man inside, in a wheelchair. He was buying cookies and trying to pay for them. I told him to give me the money, and I would pay for the cookies. He looked at me and said that he wanted me to come to his house. I had stopped standing on Gadsden and Montgomery servicing tricks before that, but I did not have God on my mind. Yet, if someone just wanted to pay me, it was fine with me. I asked my cousin for the man's address so that I could get some of his money. When I walked into his house, I asked, "Are you ready?" He said, "No, I can't do anything." I sat on the side of the wheelchair as he ate his dinner. I noticed that his pouch was hooked to the wheelchair. I asked him for $10 to get a rock (cocaine).

I had not done drugs for two years. He told me that I did not need drugs. I decided to unhook the pouch, got up, and walked out the door. Later, I was arrested. As I was lying down in jail, the Holy Spirit visited me. He told me that the truth would make me free. The detective wanted me to admit that I robbed the man. I didn't do it until I got to jail and heard that word from the Holy Spirit. When my lawyer came, I told him that I had robbed the man. That's when I surrendered my life to the Lord. When I got to court, I saw the man in the wheelchair. The District Attorney swore him in and asked him if he saw the lady who robbed him on May 29, 2010. The man said, "No, I do not." She asked him again, "Sir, I am going to ask you again whether you see the lady who snatched your money on May the 29th?" He rolled out of the courtroom. The judge, the lawyer, and the DA were astonished. The judge said, "Go out there; catch him, and bring him back." The police came back and said the man was gone. The judge told them to take me out of his courtroom.

What a day that was in my life. I was sitting in the courtroom. The man was looking at me, but he said that he did not see me. From that day on, my life was not the same. When I got back to jail, the girls asked me what happened. I told them. They thought that I was going home. I was not. I had to face the charge. I had confessed. Sentenced to prison, I was spiritually free from bondage. That's what the Holy Spirit meant when He said that the truth would make me free. That was the beginning of me surrendering my life to the Lord. While in prison, I prayed, worshiped the Lord, and told the people of His goodness. I told them that the same one who set me free could set them free - in prison.

When I was in prison, my roommate passed away in our cell. She told me that her chest hurt. I told her to tell the guards herself. They told her that she had gas and sent her back to the cell. I told her to drink some hot water and eat a little mustard, a prison remedy for gas. Playfully, I said, "If you die on me, I will kill you." I took a shower. When I came back, she was on her bed, gasping for air. She was blue. Other inmates tried to revive her, but she died. It was the first time I had seen someone die. I was devastated. I couldn't run to my mama, alcohol, or drugs. I had to run to Jesus. I continued my walk and ministered while I was in a halfway house in Atlanta. When I came home, I got a divorce for free. He didn't want to sign the papers or let me go. God said, "You're already free. You're my child now." For years, I prayed for a husband. I prayed for a God-fearing man. It took a while. That's how I felt, but my timing is not God's timing. I prayed, and I watched. I stayed sober. God sent me a husband. I waited nine years and remained celibate, the same prostitute that used to stand on Gadson and Montgomery. I said, "God keep me. Keep my sex drive, as I wait on you to send me a husband." He sent me one. The last time I gave this testimony in church, my husband was sitting there. He'll bring you out! I thank God that I can share what he has done for me!

MEET SANDRA EARVEN

Mrs. Sandra Earven is the Founder of From The Streets to The Streets. Her area of expertise is clothing, feeding and ministering to the homeless. When not hard at work Sandra enjoys singing in the choir and spending quality time with her husband.

Connect with Sandra Earven:

www.facebook.com/sandra.sampson.756

A Faith That Builds

Carletha Harris

What has got me this far in my life? Faith! Faith is simply trusting God to do what only God can do. Life can be tough. Sometimes giving up becomes a plague in your mind. Having faith somehow lifts your spirit so high until you feel you can do anything. I am a true believer. I trust and believe in God because he has restored me so many times throughout my life. I've watched so many miraculous things happen for others. I'm a true believer that no matter what your circumstances are or what path you've chosen, it's never too late to have faith. All you have to do is allow God to step into your life.

I have been led to encourage the single mothers being blessed to raise their children by themselves. I say blessed because it's a blessing to see every milestone of your children's lives. Mothers make sacrifices and modify their life to make sure their kids are well taken care of. They put dreams on hold and even their health. My situation may be different than yours, but our feelings from what we go through are the same. Growing up we all had dreams of having a family of our own, in which both parents were happy together. It doesn't always work out as planned and that's okay.

Being a single mother, I've had many obstacles I faced alone. Sometimes I had to go without just so my kids could have. There were many late nights at the table trying to do homework, cooking and only managing to get a couple hours of sleep. I want to encourage you to build your faith like I did and see how your life will turn out for the better. Every mother sometime or another has felt burnt out, depressed, stressed, overwhelmed, hopeless and even financially strained. You may feel like you're alone and the only one who is going through such things. Some people carry their load differently than others. Some suffer in silence, which leads to more harm than good and some go with the flow, which could accumulate a lot of emotions at one time. There are a lot of ways to cope with the everyday life of being a single mother. Don't think that your problems are any less important than anyone else. You must remember that you are a person and you have needs too. Being a mother is not the stem of why we feel certain emotions. We must figure out what works best for us individually. Sometimes circumstances may happen out of our control, but we have been chosen because God knew we were right for the job. It's an honor to maneuver through the struggle of being a mother. Be encouraged.

At the peak of motherhood, I saw patterns in my life as I was trying to better myself. No matter how hard I tried I was getting the same results. This repetition resulted in me getting behind in my finances. Trying to work and go to school put a strain on me. I dropped out and started my dream of modeling. I tried to do this in my spare time, however, not having a babysitter put an end to that. It seemed as if I was pushed three steps back after taking one step forward. I could never make ends meet. I was always just getting by. Most single mothers who work can never get approved for food stamps. In addition to food becoming an issue I always struggled with not having enough for childcare. I had a very good job at the time but my car was always an issue. Even though I only spent money on the necessities, I was still struggling and getting behind. Once you get behind, it's hard to get back on track because things accumulate. As I sadly sat overwhelmed, all I could do was cry. I had so much built up emotions. I had thoughts about getting a second job but that would be impossible, as I had no one to watch my kids. Even if I could work two jobs, that would consume all of my time and I would never be able to see them. This cycle went on for a few years and I sucked it up as I took out a few loans and pawned a few items and that eventually ran out. I could no longer put myself into any more debt.

Stress will make you a mess, which is what I was; a mess. I suffered being stressed out for a long time with no one knowing. I put my best face on everywhere I went. I felt like this was my journey and really did not know what anyone could do to help me. They have their own household to take care of. That is where I was wrong. I went so long feeling sorry for myself and not speaking up. I felt ashamed being swallowed by bills and struggling to put food on the table. I equated that with not being a good mother. I have a very good support system. I didn't realize that until I was left with no choice. I lost a lot by not speaking up. By speaking up and no longer feeling ashamed, I gained more than I lost.

I want to tell you a few things I've done to build my faith and get on track to becoming a better person for myself and my kids. Be encouraged. I began to do what I was always told to do while growing up. That was to begin with God. I was raised that no matter what you go through put God ahead of your life. I've always had God in my heart but I gave him a back-seat ride in my life. That is why my life was suffering and I couldn't stay leveled. My kids and I got back into church and allowed God to lead us. But what uplifted my life was when I paid my tithes. I had little to give at the time but I gave what I had. I always heard the older folks talk about tithes and giving God what is owed to him. I had to see it to believe it. Blessings on top of blessings kept coming my way. I couldn't keep up with it all. I had people come up to me and ask if they could bless my kids and I. We were sponsored for Christmas at a church where they gave us a donation. Strangers would come up to me and bless me with different things. I had friends and family who were also a blessing in so many ways it was unexplainable. I put God first and he shined a light on me that sent only blessings my way. Being blessed allowed me to be a blessing to others. On top of going to church and paying my tithes I fasted and meditated on God's word and gave him some of my time. For me to be a better person and retrieve the pieces I had lost along the way, I had to see what I was doing wrong and make better choices. What better way than to go to the source. Instead of fasting from food I would fast from things I clanged to or something that I thought I couldn't live without. I would fast from those things a few times a week or however long I felt in my spirit to do so. I would also recommend paying attention to the people you let into your circle. Being amongst positive people has always been a practice for me. Being good and respectful to others and surrounding myself with like-minded people who are a joy to be around. Others' negativity can drain your energy and knock you off balance.

There is this online mother's group that I was invited to join that gave me a lot of insight on what mother's go through. A lot of us were going through the same things. We were helping one another and building relationships. I felt so grateful to witness these ladies in action. Whenever a mother needed gas for work, pampers, baby formula or two hours to themselves, those ladies made sure they got it done. I would recommend contacting a mother's group because they can relate and they will not judge you.

Some may say being a mother is not that serious, however for me it was tough. No doubt about it, mothers are very strong but we also get worn out and tired. We stretch ourselves thin trying to do everything but we will never break. Through it all, you get to watch your children unfold like a butterfly because you never gave up. All those hugs and kisses become far, few and in between so enjoy because they grow so fast. Hold your head up and be proud to be a mother. "Being a mother is Twice the Work, Twice the Stress and Twice the Tears but also Twice the Hugs, Twice the Love and Twice the Pride''. Be encouraged.

Everything that I have talked about would not have mattered or worked if I didn't build my faith. For a while I realized that I was walking by sight and wanted to be in control of everything in my life. Growing in faith, you must stop putting limits on your life and let God take control. Also, allow yourself to have God size dreams because God is able. I managed to close on my first home as a single mom by stepping out on faith and dreaming big. I've pursued my dream of modeling and returning to school. The sky's the limit, and I must be a leader for my children. That is only the beginning of what's to come for me and my family. I'm still on my journey and I have learned so much along the way. I have ensured my kids know that God is the foundation if you want a stable life. I'm growing and learning everyday. I'm not perfect and I don't have everything in order but I do know that I'm right on track.

Everyone has something different going on in their life, some worse than others, but everyone should have faith. Mustard seed faith will produce a lifetime of blessings. Believing in what is unseen but seeing it unfold is the blessing of faith.

MEET CARLETHA HARRIS

Carletha Harris is a Patient Service Technician Specialist from Bishopville, SC. She now resides in Columbia, SC. Her home church is Gumspring Baptist Church. She is the mother of two handsome boys and a beautiful daughter. She is an aspiring model and the Brand Ambassador of House of Stone by CoCo. She has dreams to finish Esthetic School and create her own line of products. When not working, she enjoys being with family and creating her own natural hair care products. This is her first writing project with hopes of encouraging others to unlock their faith.

Connect with Carletha Harris:

www.facebook.com/carlethajharris/

Email: Carlethaharris@yahoo.com

He Shall Recover It All

Darnita Young

It was November 3, 2018 and I was walking down the aisle to marry the man that I loved. It was so familiar but so unconventional. So many were confused with our union but happy for us at the same time. The scenery was beautiful and of course I looked amazing. As I prepared myself for my vows, I couldn't help but reminisce about my first wedding. The chaos, the table without a tablecloth, the cold food, the tears and the butterflies. But this time it was different. There were no butterflies, only expectations of how God was going to move in my marriage. See, the thought of God restoring a marriage that was so irrevocably broken was a mere miracle. Even I had to ask God, "Are you sure" with a chuckle.

Marriage is God's perfect union. It is His template and design to carry you through life. It is the most important relationship you will have on this earth. Choosing the one that you will spend the rest of your life with is one of the most important decisions that you will ever make next to accepting Jesus Christ as your Lord and Savior. Marriage produces a lifelong ministry of love, children, memories, compromise and sacrifice. Your greatest wins, losses, trials, tribulations, heartbreaks, pains, happiness and joy.

All of these emotions can only be experienced with

your spouse and sometimes just because of your spouse. This is why the words for better or worse, richer or poorer, in sickness and in health, to love and to cherish until death do us part are words that can haunt those who struggle in their marriage. The thought of staying in a marriage when you don't want to seems to be torturous, unfair and useless waste of my time. Thinking to yourself I could move on with my life but; for better or worse. However, what if worse is worse, worse is annoying, and worse is stressful? What if worse is unhealthy for your children? What if worse is infidelity? What if worse is an surrendered spouse? So the real question that I had to ask myself is, do I stay in a marriage that makes me unhappy? The Bible says:

"Matthew 19:9 NKJV "And I say to you, whoever divorces his wife, except for sexual immorality, and marries another, commits adultery; and whoever marries her who is divorced commits adultery".

The reason that we know this scripture is because we are trying to find a way out, a reason to be free and a reason to validate the worse. At least I was and the worse was more than enough for me to file the divorce. I clearly remember the day that I said I was leaving. I remember the feeling of hurt, pain, disgust and failure. I remember it so clearly because this time I knew it was real. I'd said the word divorce several times before, but this time it was different. I knew this was it and it was over. So I did it, I filed for the divorce and moved on with my life. I became consumed with seeking God with more intention so that I could live in freedom and wholeness. I went to counseling through my church and I saw a therapist. I was able to talk out all the things that had been bothering me from childhood until the current day.

What I found was, I needed help. Maybe the divorce was strictly for me to become a better person. To understand who I am and why I did some of the things that I did. It was for me to become whole. As I began to walk in freedom and wholeness, it was liberating and the peace was amazing. I began to look at myself as a single woman and I started praying for my future husband as single women tend to do. I began the process of mastering difficult things like being a single mother, living on one income, going to places alone and talking about my divorce. It quickly turned into a season of unfamiliarity and fear because my life had changed so drastically. But I was determined to go through that season and win! But for some reason God wouldn't let my spirit settle. Something didn't sit well in my spirit even after the counseling and therapy. I prayed, and I cried, and I cried, and I prayed, but something wasn't right. There was still a void and I tried to fill it by keeping busy with my children, work and church. But there was still something missing. As I was praying, God was giving me visions of getting remarried to my soon to be ex-husband and my divorce wasn't even final yet. I began to think that I had to be crazy to believe that God was telling me to stay in this marriage.

After all the prayer and war rooming over this thing, getting self-care and becoming a better me, how am I supposed to go back. Nope, God, I'm still not feeling it. So I rebelled against the thought of reconciliation. I was praying for my future husband, not my current husband. I tried to forget about it and move on with my life. It was clear to me that it wasn't the right time to even have the discussion of reconciliation. It just seemed so silly. God are you forsaking me? I released him from the bondage of me. All that he says that I am and the things he says that I do, he is now released from. So why am I not at peace? HE IS FREE TO BE HAPPY! So why am I in bondage, why can't I be free? The reality is, that while I felt as if I was moving on with my life, God was preparing me for the unexpected. So I stepped back to evaluate if this was God or me. I began praying diligently so that I could make sure that I was hearing the voice of the Lord and not my own. I realized that the Lord loves me so much that He will give me confirmation over and over again. Even in my inability to be obedient to His word, He was still working things out for my good. I once thought God didn't work out the messy things in our lives until I read the story of Hosea and Gomer:

"Then the Lord said to me again, "Gomer has many lovers, but you must continue loving her. Do this because it is an example of the Lord's love for Israel. He continues to love them, but they continue to turn to other

gods…" (Hosea 3:1 ERV)

Now, I know what you are thinking, NO, I did not have many lovers but we did have circumstances that seemed unrecoverable. Just like Hosea, God had to speak to me several times about our reconciliation. But if the Lord could speak to Hosea and tell him to get his wife while she was committing adultery by living with another man then my situation was small in comparison. What I have found is that the word of God is true and when we feel like God is not moving, He is working on our behalf through His own timing, even if we believe it or not.

"And we know that all things work together for good to those who love God, to those who are called according to His purpose" (Romans 8:28 NKJV). "The Lord is not being slow in doing what he promised—the way some people understand slowness. But God is being patient with you. He doesn't want anyone to be lost. He wants everyone to change their ways and stop sinning" (2 Peter 3:9 ERV).

God desires for each and everyone of us to have a fulfilling marriage. A marriage where we put Him first and where He gets the glory out of our relationships. He wants us to have a marriage with purpose. No matter the circumstances, He wants to recover it all; all that was lost! But we need to invite Him into our marriages so that He can repair them. I was ready, and I heard from the Lord. I was ready to move forward with staying in my marriage but to my surprise he wasn't. So I set myself up to believe that we were supposed to be together, and he decides he wants to move on with his life. The heartbreak was devastating, but I dealt with it. So God, now what? I'm tired of putting my life on hold, can I please move on? I did what you told me to do and I'm sure I missed the mark, but it's OK. I will move on and this will be a thing of the past. I proceeded with finalizing the divorce. I pretended like I was fine and tried to live at peace with it. Even though I tried my best to move on, circumstances kept pulling me back like a magnet. But by this time the divorce was final and I was ready to move on with my life and maybe get a boyfriend. Who does God have for me? I had been praying for my future husband, and I was even praying that my ex would get a wife that would support him and take good care of our kids. I prayed that he would be the perfect mate and father for our children. I was doing all the right things, so boyfriend where you at? Ha, ha, ha. I didn't seem to meet the person that was right for me. Dating was not in my future. Which I didn't understand because I really thought I was doing everything right. So I decided that the single life would be fine. As the year went on, I continued to cultivate my relationship with Christ and didn't worry about anything else. But here comes that magnet again and I can't seem to get away.

Is this just a soul tie or is this God? So once again, I started praying and God started revealing to me the steps

I needed to take. Pray for specific things, be patient during this time because it's not going to look like what I think it should. Wait until the time is right and pose the question for restoration, but not until then. Unfortunately, it was a sensitive conversation for both of us. So I waited and observed, I began to see the signs. Then it hit me, we still loved each other, but the process of reconciliation was not easy. We were so broken about the past and worried about us being the same people in the future. This concern seemed to rule all of our conversations. "I can't do this God". I want it to be easy and I want a true love story. But God said, "I want restoration." Things won't always look like we want them to.

The restoration conversation was full of tears and heartbreak. We had to discuss the pain of the past to get to the future, and it hurt. Regardless of what people say, time doesn't heal all wounds, but time does allow you to forget how bad it hurts. But when you revisit those feelings, the pain seems to intensify like it happened just yesterday. So we worked through the pain and decided that we were getting remarried even after all the chaos and craziness. We prayed together, we did a marriage bible study, we went to counseling and we went to a marriage workshop. We had to do all of that before anyone would even marry us. All of these tools helped us in many ways. But we still had to make vows to each other. Promises that we would be different, that we would be better, but first and foremost, we would put

God first in our marriage. Hosea said to Gomer:

"I said to her, "You are to live with me for many days. You must not be promiscuous or belong to any man, and I will act the same way toward you" (Hosea 3:3 CSB).

He was saying, you change your ways and so will I. The intention is that I got you back now; let's do what it takes to stay together. That's what marriage is, a union where each person works at it every day until you both look at each other as God does, "The Apple of His Eye." When we see each other as God does, it's easier to forgive one another, it's easier to pray for one another and it's easier to be a confidant partner. It's easier to become one flesh when we put God first. So we did it, we got remarried in front of friends and family. Some thought we were crazy, some were just supporters, some thought it was a miracle and some are still waiting for the destruction of the second time around. But who cares why they were there. We made vows to God once again and we will fight to keep them this time around.

"So then, they are no longer two but one flesh. Therefore what God has joined together, let not man separate"(Matthew 19:6 NKJV).

What I learned about marriage restoration is that it is not easy, it is hard work and that the work does not end when you say, "I do" that's when it begins. If you are struggling in your marriage, restoration will be difficult until you can do these four things.

Forget - *"Forget the former things; do not dwell on the past" (Isaiah 43:18 NIV).*

Forgive - *"And be kind to one another, tenderhearted, forgiving one another, even as God in Christ forgave you" (Ephesians 4:32 NKJV).*

Trust - *"Trust in the LORD with all your heart, And lean not on your own understanding" (Proverbs 3:5 NKJV).*

Love - *"But God demonstrates His own love toward us, in that while we were still sinners, Christ died for us" (Romans 5:8 NKJV).*

I am working daily to forget the past, forgive prior indiscretions, trusting that I am walking in God's perfect plan and loving my husband unconditionally. It is work and it takes unshakable faith! But it's also very rewarding to know that God has a plan for my marriage, and I am instrumental in ensuring that the plan comes to pass. *A man's heart plans his way, but the Lord directs his steps. (Proverbs 16:9 NKJV).* So even when I get discouraged I know that God is directing my steps and I remember that with God all things are possible. There is nothing too hard for Him to do. He will never leave me nor forsake me, and He loved me enough to restore my marriage, therefore; He Shall Recover It All!

"I will repay you for the years the locusts have eaten— the great locust and the young locust, the other locusts and the locust swarm — my great army that I sent among

you. You will have plenty to eat until you are full, and you will praise the name of the Lord your God, who has worked wonders for you; never again will my people be shamed" (Joel 2:25-26 NIV).

MEET DARNITA YOUNG

Darnita Young, a busy wife, mother, author, blogger, entrepreneur and vision mentor. Her mission is to encourage, empower and equip busy women with tools that will catapult their lives to the next level. Darnita is passionate about sharing the love of Christ, Vision and Prayer. She is the author of "Pray in the Midst of the Hustle" Prayer Journal which is a testament of her desire to encourage others to pray, seek God in a greater way and walk in God's vision for their lives.

Connect with Darnita Young:

Instagram: @pleadingmom

Website: www.pleadingmom.com

True Insight

Dr. Nicckay Natson

The eyes of your understanding being enlightened; that ye may know what the hope of his calling is, and what the riches of the glory of his inheritance in the saints.
Ephesian 1:18 KJV

My grandmother raised my sister and me from birth. She eventually adopted us to keep us from being passed around and not be a ward of the state. I wasn't raised in the church. However, my grandmother would have discussions with my sister and me about the Bible and the Lord. I could count on my fingers how often we went to church. She would allow us to go to church with our next-door neighbor sometimes. My grandmother would sew our dresses and fix our hair nicely. We would go over to Mrs. Johnson, our neighbor's house, to show off her handy work on Easter. When we got to the church, I remember it being really loud and people running around, falling, rolling on the floor and speaking in these weird languages.

As a child this looked crazy and scared me. I would hide under Mrs. Johnson's long dress to escape all the chaos. When we got back home my grandmother would ask how was church? I can remember telling her, mom, I think something is wrong with those people in that church. My grandmother would laugh and say, baby it's okay. On the weekends we would go over to my cousin's house. My sister and I would enjoy going over there. Our cousin lived in the woods. At least that's what it seemed like to me. She lived in a big brick home with several fireplaces with huge mantles. I can remember having to look up to view the top of them. I would climb up on a chair to reach whatever was on top of the fireplace. My cousin would say, Oooooooh, you're going to get in trouble momma said that we are not supposed to play with that.

My mom said those jars have the soul of people inside of them. She put a curse on them and had their souls trapped. As a child, I had no idea what she was talking about. Inside, the jars look really weird to me. They contained a clear substance with filthy film floating in the center. I remember when she told me that, I could see the faces of two black men and a white woman flash in front of my eyes. I told my cousin that there were two men and a woman inside those jars. However, I wasn't curious enough to discover more. It scared me when I saw those people's faces pop in front of me.

I can also remember my grandmother bringing my uncle to my cousin's house because he would crawl around on the ground like a snake. He lived under the house and wouldn't come in. I remember this day so vividly in my mind, it's almost like I can touch it. My family took my uncle in a back room and told all the children to go out. Forbidding us to come back in and reminding us to stay out of grown folk's business. We went outside and played while also discussing the incident with my uncle. I wanted to know what was going on. Why did he behave the way he did and why was he living under the house?

They were in the house for a long time and when they finally came out my uncle was put in the bed so he could rest. My cousin and I snuck into the room where my uncle was resting. When we entered the room nothing was there except a white bucket that looked like an old paint can. I looked inside the bucket. I will never forget what I saw. I saw this snail-like thing with a body, but it was something else. It would stretch out and go back together. It was huge. Until this day I have seen nothing else like that on earth. I heard the grown-ups talking about it. My aunt whom I discovered was a witch doctor, helped to get that snail-like thing out of him. That thing I saw had him crawling around like a snake and living underneath the house.

After the incident with my uncle I discovered more about my family and why they were so secretive. People from all over the world would come to my aunt for her to remove roots, curses, spells and voodoo off of them. Every now and then when someone would hurt one of our family members intentionally their souls would be trapped "in the between". I learned that my entire family on my grandmothers' side was gifted with sight they could see and foretell the future. Many people would come to hear what their future holds. My grandmother could also tell them their past and present.

While growing up when I would see things I was told that I was crazy and there was something wrong with me. I discovered my aunts were gifted women. Before my Godfather died I told my grandmother he was dead. She told me not to say it and ten minutes afterwards the phone rang and she was informed that he had passed. She looked at me and asked, how I knew that. I knew because he told me. He is standing in the hallway. When I would see things and disclose what I saw, I was told; something was wrong with me.

As a child I could feel and sense when things were not right in places, people and even with objects. I would say that object has something wrong with it and you shouldn't buy that. I would have visitations from angels. Angelic hosts would visit me often as a child. I would see so many beautiful lights with many colors and I would dream, dreams of heaven. I could also see demons and things of darkness. When I was 12-years-old, I got sick with double pneumonia. By the time my grandmother discovered that I was sick, it was too late. He gave me medications to take but told my grandmother it was nothing he could do.

At 12-years-old, I died on that bed. I remember it like it was yesterday. I could see a light as I was traveling through this tunnel-like thing with a lot of figures on each side. I couldn't see the figures or make out who they were. I felt so much peace and comfort as I was going toward the light. I can remember looking back and seeing myself lying on the bed. They kept saying go toward the light. As I walked in the direction of the light, I heard my grandmother say no, in the name of Jesus, come back. When my grandmother said that my body shifted and turned me around. I could feel my spirit being pulled back into my body at a fast rate.

When I came back into my body, I opened my eyes. When I opened my eyes I saw a tall bright figure standing beside my bed. I tried to see the face but the light was too bright for me. After that incident I was healed and within two days I was feeling good again. After five complete days I was back on my feet running around playing. This is not my only experience with that. I remember a time when my mother tried to kill me by submerging me underwater while I was still asleep.

Growing up I had envisioned and experienced so many things that no child should have to experience. I heard about this God. My grandmother used to tell us about Him and as she read the Bible to us. We as a family never went to church. We never experienced the presence of the God of Abraham, Jacob and Isaac, as she would say. At 12-years-old I had many supernatural experiences, including my uncle being delivered and my physical death and restoration. I was too young to know what faith was or what faith was all about. My grandmother would say it all the time; you must have faith. I dreamed about heaven, I had visitations from angels and I was in the presence of God as a child but didn't understand what was happening. I thought it was normal for all children to experience the things I experienced. To see what I saw and feel what I felt. As I got older I began to discover this thought was incorrect.

We are different. God made us all unique. Each individual person has their own path and process in life they have to go through. As I matured there were things I experienced and saw that I would talk to the Lord about. As a child I would ask the Lord to give me faith. Growing up into adulthood I would ask the Lord for more faith in Him. This was before I had a real true authentic relationship with Him and before I knew what faith was.

In my junior year in high school I met my high school sweetheart whom I am married to today, Alton T. Natson. We have been married for 23 years. He introduced me to the Lord. I had no example of the bride and the bridegroom; I had a form of godliness growing up. The people in my family lacked a true relationship with Him. Once I gave my life to Christ through faith my eyes were opened to a lot of things within my family. God had given me true authentic insight. That is when the Lord began to Father me and fill the void of me not having a father in my life.

When I first got saved the Lord would visit me often

in dreams and share secrets and give me insight. Before I was saved I had a dream that the Lord told me I was called and chosen as his Prophet. He told me in the dream, I have set you this day over nations and over kingdoms, to pluck up and to break down, to destroy and to overthrow, to build and to plant. *Jeremiah 1:10*. That I was called to win souls, those that are in a desolate place. I didn't know what a Prophet was until years later. The Lord would confirm through other Prophets.

God had to take me out from my family and all the things that were familiar to me to truly deliver me from bondage. He set me free from my past so that I would be a generational curse bloodline breaker. What I was introduced to growing up was all that my family had known. As a child I was different, I was set apart and chosen by God. I had visitations by angelic host and God-inspired dreams, while family members cussed, got drunk, used drugs, was abusive, operated in witchcraft and works of the flesh. The Lord re-calibrated my eyes to see through dove's eyes; eyes that see through the Spirit of the Living God. He breathes his breath upon my sight and mind. My relationship with the Lord became intimate by spending more time with Him and that is when I discovered I had the gift of faith.

This faith was different from the *Hebrews 11:1* faith: *Now faith is the substance of things hoped for and the evidence of things not seen.* The gift of faith goes beyond that. I have seen God work miracles and do the impossible in my life and the lives of others as I pray and release my faith to believe God for them. Whatever you believe God for right now at this very moment, hold on to the faith. Don't give up! You are on the cusp of greatness. You are at the brink of your red sea. With the rod of Moses and with my faith attached we shall smite the water and whatever your red sea is, you will cross over to the other side. It took great faith to endure and become resilient after seeing all that I saw, knowing all that I know and great faith not to have crazy come up on me.

It took my grandmother's great faith for that miracle to be performed with me. Today, God uses me to perform miracles and the miraculous comes through my vessel. I am submitted and yielded to God, not because I am such a great person. It's because of who He is in my life. If you have experienced things as a child, seen things or felt things, just know that you are not crazy. Keep the faith and trust in God to help carry you through it. Grow closer to God, get in an intimate place with Him and He will lead you to a person that can help you. Because of my faith a great ministry has been birthed out of me. Ask God to increase your faith and greatness will be birthed out of you too.

Igniting Your Faith Prayer

Father In the name of Jesus I thank you for your love, mercy and kindness that you have toward me. I want to know you on a deeper level. I want to be intimate with you, Lord. Enlighten the eyes of my understanding. Give me true insight into what's going on around me. Don't let me be blind to the enemy's devices. Help me to understand who I am in you, give me clarity on my identity in you. Set your Holy Fire all around me. Set my soul on fire for you. Abba, I ask that you re-ignite my faith in you. Increase my capacity for more faith. Allow me to go through and experience the miraculous because of my faith. The faith I have in the Almighty. Let me enjoy the peace of being in your presence daily. I surrender my will, emotions and intellect over unto you. Have your way in my life Lord. Fill me up with your Spirit. Holy Spirit set me on fire. Let me ignite the fire in others as the fire within me is ignited. In Jesus Name, Amen.

MEET DR. NICCKAY NATSON

Dr. Nicckay Natson is also a Prophet and Apostle of God at Alton and Nicckay Natson Ministries (ANNM), Kingdom Alliance Global Network and the upcoming church plant will be located in Atlanta, Georgia. Dr. Nicckay's heart is to see the kingdom of God released in the earth. Her areas of expertise are inner healing, counseling, leadership, mentorship and training, building and foundations, writing grants, creativity, financial management, business and entrepreneurship. Before she started her own business Dr. Nicckay served in various arenas for the government for 20 years. Dr. Nicckay enjoys spending time with her family and being a glam-ma. Dr. Nicckay is married to her husband of 24 years, Apostle Alton Natson.

Connect with Dr. Nicckay Natson:

Website: www.drnicckaynatson.com

Facebook: Dr. Nicckay Natson @RemnantArising

Twitter: @Destin4Greater

Instagram: Dr. Nicckay Natson

#SimplyFaith

Pastor Chris & Prophetess Barbara Wells

"Now faith is the substance of things hoped for, the evidence of things not seen." Hebrews 11:1 (KJV)

The just shall live by faith! FAITH, is definitely how we learned to live!

Prophetess Barbara:

In the small city of Earle, Arkansas is where it all began. My husband and I and our two beautiful children resided in a small two-bedroom mobile home. We lived there for eight years, it may not have been much to others, but it was home to us. We were grateful! Where we felt there was no hope, God always came through and provided a way. Even though my seven-year-old son and nine-year-old daughter were in school my plate was still full as a working mom. It was a balancing act to be a full-time working wife with additional responsibilities.

Somehow I managed to minister, cook, clean, and still help my children with their homework. Despite it all I still found time to spend with my Heavenly Father. Praying day in and day out, keeping the faith in our Lord, was my strength despite our circumstances! My husband was working at a major trucking company in Memphis, TN. He was the Shop Manager for five and a half years. He supervised the transportation department. He was responsible for the upkeep of all the trucks and trailers.

Being Shop Manager, he was bringing home a decent paycheck. With God at the forefront, things were going pretty well. I heard an elderly lady once say, "pretty good" is hard to beat. With us both working 12-hour days, five to six days a week with only one mode of transportation, it was tough! We'd get the kids off to the sitter to catch the bus to school. I would drop my husband off at his job between 6:00-6:30 and be at work by 7:00. This was a daily routine because we had no one we could depend on for transportation. As you know, people are not willing to help much these days.

In March of 2006, I went into the hospital for foot surgery, which put me off work for about a month. I already knew I would be off for a while. I really didn't care, because I was undecided about returning anyway. We had always stated we wanted to start our own business. With the knowledge and credentials we both had; why not! You already know what happened. I didn't go back. I stayed home to take care of my babies. Boy, were they glad! They had missed my attendance at all of their school functions and also missed having dinner ready when they returned from school. Plus, they didn't like being at the sitter anyway. Ha! They had their mommy back for a little while!

Pastor Chris:

In May 2006, I got up one morning and headed to work, feeling good and blessed. What I thought would be a normal day turned out to be tragic! I arrived at work, and my boss met me at the door. He stated, "This is it." I asked, "What do you mean?'' He said, "we are closing up this facility right now for good." I was stunned and asked why. He couldn't give me a good reason, so I asked for a second time. "Why?" He still couldn't give me an accurate reason. He told me to pack my belongings and leave as soon as possible. I had no idea what was happening or what I was going to do. I had a wife and two kids to take care of. Tears fell down my face. I had no idea how I was going to break this news to my wife, but God knows I had to tell her. In such few words, she said, "Trust God!" Those few words helped to ease my pain. Bless God!

In June of that year, we started our own tractor/trailer mechanic business. We started with an old 1987 Ford pickup. God gave us what we needed to rebuild. We turned this pickup truck into our service truck. God opened many doors for this little company. Small, but big in heart! She went to work with me every day and worked on the trucks alongside me. Hot, cold, good or bad. She hung in there. All we had was each other and God. It wasn't easy, but as stated in Matthew 19:26 - With God all things are possible! I thank God for my beautiful wife sticking by my side. Praying over me when I thought all hope was lost. She encouraged me to hold on, telling me we will make it. We did!

When things slowed down in the business I worked

for others driving their trucks. I was both the driver and mechanic yet underpaid. My wife stated she was tired of me driving and working on someone else's truck and not being compensated for it. She said, "With your potential, we should have our own." We stepped out on faith to purchase our own truck. The first truck we had in mind was a dump truck. We had no money to start this business, so we went to the bank for a loan. God blessed my lovely wife to put together her first business plan. One banker said it was the best, most well put together business plan he ever laid eyes on. He then said we are millionaires. Only to turn around and say, "I'm sorry, but I can't help you." Really!? After all that and the answer was still no. My God will allow you to go through certain situations in life to see where you stand in your faith! Can you trust Him when it seems all hell is breaking loose?

Pastor Chris & Prophetess Barbara Wells:

We went from bank to bank and still heard no after no. We began to wonder if we were ever going to hear the word "Yes!" It was so depressing, and we felt that no one would help us. We prayed and labored before God. We decided we were going to give it one last try and we were done! If it didn't work this time, it's obviously not meant to be. Someone told us about a place that sells trucks, which was two hours away from our home. We went down and looked at them and picked one out. The owner sent us to their bank to see if we qualify for a loan.

When we arrived we did not know what to expect. We had less than perfect credit and no money for a down payment. We knew what we were up against but we decided that we would still go.

Despite not knowing the outcome we still wanted to try. Of course, we were nervous because we didn't want to hear no again. We entered the bank with confidence. The banker ran both our credit reports. When he came back into the room his face was red. He had to pull off his glasses and wipe his forehead from sweating. We looked at each other like, uh oh. He said, "Now y'all know your credit is messed up, don't ya?" Our scores were in the fours and fives. He stated that he would not be able to do anything. We looked at each other and said, we are not going through this again. We began praying and talking to the Father. He asked us to hold on, as he left the room. We said, we are not leaving here without that truck. God didn't bring us this far to leave us now. The banker walked back in and sat down. He saw that we were not giving up on this truck, and he noticed the confident look on our faces. He said, "We are going to give y'all a chance." Hallelujah, thank you Jesus! You came through. When things were looking down, we kept looking up. When we felt like giving up, we kept the faith. When man said no, God said yes!

We finally purchased our first Semi-Truck and started our trucking company. Eleven years later we have a brand-new Dump Truck, a Semi (Tractor & Trailer),

Bobcat Skid Steer, another Service Truck and multiple trucks working under our authority. We also contract on State and Federal jobs along with many other major companies. We have two Clothing Lines, a New Shoe Line, two Ministries and much more to come. This is only a snippet of where God has brought us from and where He's taking us. Be on the lookout for our full life story coming soon. No matter what things may look like, keep the faith and don't give up. There is nothing too hard for God! *BUT WITHOUT FAITH IT IS IMPOSSIBLE TO PLEASE HIM: Hebrews 11:6 KJV*

MEET PASTOR CHRIS & PROPHETESS BARBARA WELLS

Pastor Chris and Prophetess Barbara Wells are the Founders of A Faithful Few Ministry and Radical 4 Christ. They are the CEO's of D & D Wells Trucking LLC, and Fashion Brands Modesti and Azzarri Couture. Their areas of expertise include Ministry, Motivational Speaking, Poetry, Fashion and Designing. When not hard at work, Chris & Barbara enjoy ministering, spending quality time together at dinner/a movie, quality time with their precious grandbabies, building and designing cars and vacationing.

Connect with Pastor Chris and Prophetess Barbara Wells:

Facebook.com/BarbaraRobinsonWells and Instagram at Modesti3d

The Filmmaker With Unshakable Faith

Laura Poindexter

A Memoir:

Before she became an actress, producer, director and multi-award winning screenwriter, Laura "Kim" Poindexter was on a path of self-destruction. Notoriously known by her middle name "Kim" she was full of pain, anger, hate and rage. These tumultuous feelings would fester over the years, causing her to fight a losing battle against the many demons in her life.

Her first memories of life; began with death. Prior to the death of her mother she had no memories at all. To be fair, she was only six years old at the time. There is a phenomenon known as childhood amnesia. This is a common form of amnesia, which causes us to forget our earlier childhood memories. Around the age of six years old our brains begin to build the memory board. Thus, her very first permanent memory would be the death of her mother. She would not be able to remember her mother's smile. Nor did she have any fond memories to cleave to. The only thing she could or would remember concerning her mother is loss and death. The person who loves her the most, was gone forever.

She blamed God for her mother's death, and wanted to know why He would allow such a thing to happen. As she grew up, everything she attempted to do was overshadowed by the pain of her mother's death, despite knowing God, growing up in the church, singing in the choir and being baptized in the Holy Spirit. It would be a long hard road to true salvation and a relationship with God. She would eventually experience the greatest love of all in Jesus Christ. However, she would first have to deal with the Post Traumatic Stress Disorder (PTSD) that stemmed from her mother's untimely passing.

Initially she had high hopes that her father would swoop in like a black superhero and fix everything. As it turns out, he needed his wife just as much as she needed her mother. This revelation was confirmed when her father announced that she would be moving in with her grandmother and he would not be joining her. Losing two parents at one time was more than she could bear. She was confused, bitter and especially angry. Between the ages of fourteen and twenty-seven she would become a part of life's underbelly. Her environment (New York City) would provide fertile soil for her demons to thrive. The safety of her two-parent household had been replaced with a caring grandmother who was unfortunately married to a raging drunk. Despite her grandmother's dedication to raise her in a safe and loving environment, her best efforts were overshadowed by her husband's drunkard tirades. Her father would continue to live his life and become one of Harlem's biggest drug dealers. She would struggle to live her life and go on to become one of Harlem's biggest drug addicts. Doing whatever it took to get the next hit.

Her many near death experiences caused family members and onlookers alike to question if she even understood the meaning of "rock bottom." Her moment of reckoning was the day she discovered she was pregnant. This was the first time she felt or connected with anything in years. She would get clean for the sake of her unborn child, but returned to the street before his first birthday. Her grandmother would become her son's caretaker. It looked as if she was doomed to a life of addiction. Until one day she had a very unexpected visit from her aunt, who was a pastor. It was time to see if life was ready to deal her a new hand. If so, would she play her cards accordingly?

Her aunt offered her the opportunity to move to Baltimore, MD. to get her life on track. Her family insisted that she leave her son behind until she gained her footing. After celebrating one year of sobriety she returned to NY, to pick up her son. She would soon discover that she was ill equipped to be a mother. Determined to provide for him, she returned to the street. She would easily transition into the position of drug dealer. Selling the very same drug that destroyed her life. Not even recognizing the generational curse that was upon her. She quickly made a name for herself. However, like all of the drug dealers before her, she would rise and fall.

In 1995 faced with a prison sentence for interstate transportation of a CDS, transportation of drug manufacturing materials and the risk of losing her son; it was game over! She appeared before a judge who had the wisdom to see who she really was, but most importantly this judge could see who she was meant to be. She believes that this judge was an angel in disguise. She spoke with holy authority. Instead of sentencing her, she gave her hope. The judge spoke to her past, present and future. By the time she finished speaking the entire courtroom was in tears. This was a true, God sent, life changing opportunity to really start over. “Kim” would have to die in order for Laura to live her life and walk in her destiny. Laura would have to trust God and lean not toward her own understanding. Step by step, day-by-day, week-by-week and month-by-month, until the months turned into years.

When it was all said and done, Laura would have dedicated over twenty years of her life serving her community as a Health and Human Services Professional. Working with repeat offenders, the homeless, substance abusers and Veterans. She would performed her job with passion; the passion of Christ. Starting at the bottom, as a front desk receptionist. She would excel to Executive, Administrative Management in the field of Service. Throughout her career she would work for Drug Court, The Veterans Administration and Johns Hopkins Center for Social Concern.

In 2010 she would face another life altering event that would again challenge her faith. Similar to her mother's death, it was sudden, unexpected and out of her control. Between 2010 and 2014 Laura would lose her job, business, husband, houses, cars and was on the verge of losing her mind. Her previous experiences had taught her that the battle was not hers. She knew that God had not brought her thus far to leave her, but the place she found herself in was lonely and dark. She reminded herself that Mercy and Grace abounded. She asked God what he wanted her to do. He answered her with one word; write.

Confused and quite annoyed with the Lord's response, she was disobedient at first. However, the Lord did not relent. After two years of unsuccessfully attempting to resume her former life, she would finally follow the Lord's commands. This is when He changed her name to Laura "TheSoulWriter" Poindexter. Laura truly understands that life, circumstances and people change but God will always remain the same. Laura took all of her pain, all of her loss and all of her faith to pen her multi-award winning screenplay "Choose This Day." Being transparent about her life while writing this screenplay proved to be therapy for her and inspiration for others. She recounts her decision to move to Atlanta, GA. at fifty years old to begin the new chapter of her life. This was one of the most courageous moves she has ever made. Stating "I did not know what to expect, I was just being obedient to the voice of God. All I know is, I had to trust the process. I had to have "Unshakable Faith."

This act of obedience proved to be a true blessing. Whether she is in front of, or behind the camera she is unapologetically raw. Possessing a realness that people are drawn to. Her first film Choose This Day - The Prequel, is a movie short/music video. In addition to being the writer, Laura produced, directed and hand selected the entire cast. Unshakable Faith Productions became a licensed, registered, production company in the state of Georgia in 2019. Laura plans to continue creating written works that will inspire and tap into the deepest recesses of human emotions.

MEET LAURA POINDEXTER

Laura is a fifty-four-year old mother and grandmother with over thirty-four years of sobriety. Originally from Harlem, NY she now resides in Atlanta, GA. She is an Actress, Producer, Director and Multi-Award Winning Screenwriter. Her screenplay CTD has garnered three Official Selections and two wins. In March 2020, Laura received two Peoples Choice Nominations from The International Christian Film & Music Festival, one nomination for best Screenwriter and another for best Actress of the Year. You can see her on Netflix, Amazon, The CW and other independent movie projects. Laura often works as a freelance business contractor. Laura's life is a testament to the power of

God through His Son Jesus Christ.

Connect with Laura Poindexter:

https://filmfreeway.com/laurapoindexter

imdb.me/Laurak.Poindexter

www.facebook.com/LauraTheSoulWriter

www.facebook.com/LauraTheEntertainer

www.instagram.com/thesoulwriter1

www.youtube.com/user/GodsSoulWriter

Unshakablefaithproductions@gmail.com

On The Battlefield For The Lord

Aaron Woodson

I was born and raised in Vallejo, California, the son of Shirley Wallace and Robert Woodson. I am the proud grandson of Ernest Wallace, Fannie Wallace, Leroy Woodson Sr. and Frances Woodson. I'm proud of the village and my heritage. I graduated from Vallejo High School in 2001. Shortly after that, I enlisted in the U.S. Air Force. Before I shipped out for boot camp in San Antonio, Texas, I was involved in a terrible car accident. My friend at the time was driving and I was the passenger. My friend lost control of the Mercedes Benz car we were in. The car flipped three times and we crashed on Interstate 80. I was fortunate to suffer only minor injuries.

I remember my family came to visit me in the hospital. I was worried that I would not be able to serve in the military. They told me I would be alright and that God was watching over me. He watched over me that day and so many others too. I am thankful that my life was spared on that fateful night and I continued my journey. I joined the U.S. Air Force and served for eight years. In 2009, I enlisted in the U.S. Air National Guard and served in New Mexico for seven years. As an Operation Iraqi Freedom Combat Veteran that served two tours in both Iraq and Kuwait, I know God protected me in foreign lands with His mighty hand.

I survived an attempted mortar attack in 2006 at Camp Bucca, Iraq. I was conducting detainee operations in the detention facility with my Quick Response Force (QRF) Team. We heard a loud whistling noise in the air. Our training kicked in and we realized we needed to take cover. We did and my team immediately responded to the scene. Thankfully, none of our friends were harmed or killed. I have always been God-fearing even in my youth while being raised in the church. I used to go to church with my mom and grandma often. My family instilled strong values and morals in my character. I'm blessed to have had a strong and solid foundation in my life. I knew I needed God and I was nothing without Him. God has given me tremendous favor. He has kept me and blessed me by answering my prayers. I always desired to have a wife. I believe God will answer my prayer and give me the desires of my heart. I will have a Proverbs 31 woman that will be my wife. I'm so grateful and overjoyed by how God works things out for our good. I've gone through many storms, had many losses, been through various trials and yet God remained faithful. I pledged my allegiance and loyalty to God because He is everything I could ever want and need.

I love God with all my mind, heart, body and soul. He gets all honor and praise. I am a living witness that God can do anything. God allowed me to publish my first book called The Face of Expression in 2018. I am proud to be a published author. I am working on the sequel to my first book to be finished in May 2020. I've completed my audio book for "The Face of Expression." In my publication, I share intimate expressions about life, love, struggle, pain, faith, and relationships. You can find "The Face of Expression" on the Amazon website. Ladies and gentlemen this has been my testimony!

MEET AARON WOODSON

Aaron Woodson is a law enforcement officer at the Mayo clinic. His areas of expertise include military training tactics, networking and publishing books. When not hard at work he enjoys traveling, dancing and boxing.

Connect with Aaron Woodson:

Instagram: WOODROCK_707

I Survived

Elder Lenore Mason

I was leaving the hospital from visiting a friend, and the Lord spoke and said, "Get ready, you are going to be working here at this hospital." I responded to the Lord and said, "What will I be doing here? I am not a nurse. I don't have any medical experience."

It all started one cold day in December 2010. I had just been hired for a new job that I did not qualify for as I had no hospital experience. All I had was medical terminology knowledge from a college course I had taken in 2004. I was excited that God had opened this door for me. I arrived at my first orientation class. I had been sitting taking notes for about four hours and suddenly I felt feverish, as though I was coming down with a cold or something. I had sniffles and chills. About another hour had gone by when the trainer said, "Lenore you don't look so well let's end the orientation here and pick up on Monday." I was so thankful, I wanted to go home and lay down.

During that weekend my symptoms grew worse each day. I could not lay flat on my back without having trouble breathing, having to prop multiple pillows behind me or sleep sitting up. I coughed and choked all night barely getting any sleep. I decided on Sunday night I was going to the emergency room. After a chest X-Ray, which showed my lungs were clear, I was medicated for the flu and sent home. I arrived at work/orientation on Monday and again my trainer thought I didn't look so well and sent me home. I returned to the emergency room only to be sent home again with different medications. Upon the fourth return to the emergency room, I was then admitted to the hospital after the results of a CAT scan revealed pneumonia. My right lung was filled with fluid/infection, and my airway was closed.

The doctors came into my room to give me the results and to tell me their plan. The plan was to insert three chest tubes to drain the fluid from my lungs. I asked the doctor when would this procedure take place and he told me immediately. While the doctor was still talking, the medical staff came in with the equipment needed to perform the treatment. Everything was happening so fast. Their sense of urgency alerted me to the seriousness of the situation. In my hospital room right at my bedside, a small incision was made on my right side with no anesthetics. I had no time to pray, call my family or no time to do anything but sign the permission-to-treat form. My mind was racing, and my faith shaken - you better believe it was. The medical team announced, "at the count of three, ONE, TWO, THREE."

It seemed as if they jabbed those tubes into my side. I screamed at the top of my lungs and pulled my knees up to my chest because the pain was excruciating. The nurse requested that I stop screaming because the doctors could accidentally puncture my lung. " Not wanting to cause anymore damage to my health I managed to calm my fear. I put my legs down and bore the pain. Now the waiting began. I sat frantically hoping that the fluid would drain. Unfortunately, at about 8 p.m. the doctor came into my room to inform me that the fluid was not draining. Since the fluid was not draining, the next plan of action would be to perform emergency surgery. Immediately I talked to the Lord and asked if this sickness was unto my death. I felt like I might be dying because of the seriousness of the illness. The surgery I had was called a thoracotomy.

A thoracotomy is performed under general anesthesia. Once asleep, a breathing tube is placed into the airway to allow each lung to be separately inflated during surgery. You are then positioned on your side and an incision approximately six-inches in length is made below the bottom tip of the shoulder blade. This area is located typically between the fifth and sixth ribs. The surgeon informed me he had to use his hands to remove all the infection from my lungs after going in through my rib cage. While lying on the operating table, not sure if I would survive, yet I believed in the power of prayer. I asked a friend to say a prayer for me - weak in my own strength, still short of breath, but I had faith in the God who created me.

Thanks, be unto God I made it to recovery. Each day was challenging. Taking short breaths, I could barely breathe. I could only speak but a whisper and to inhale was the most difficult thing to do; something we take for granted. I had to actually think about breathing. All along experiencing the different emotions such as helplessness, knowing there was nothing I could do to make myself better. I had to rely on God even after the surgery. It had become a waiting game. Was the surgery successful? Was the fluid now going to drain after removing the infection? These were my thoughts. Now the spirit of depression had entered. I could do nothing for myself. I needed help performing simple, daily tasks we all take for granted. Things like going to the restroom and taking a shower were a chore. Barely able to breathe, I knew I was dying and the question arose in my heart. "Lord, you told me I would start working at this hospital, but did I get hired to get sick and die?" By this time, everyone heard the news that I was in the hospital and had surgery. It appears the entire town came to visit me. I lived in a small town and we were all like family, everyone came together in times like this.

My Pastor and First Lady came to visit and prayed for me. Other Pastors and Clergy in the community came to visit and also prayed with me. As each person visited, I could hear the whispers of some saying to the person next to them "she's dying." I even heard my brother when he walked outside my room tell his wife, "my sister is dying, I can't take this right now." He had lost his nine-year-old son approximately two months prior. My youngest daughter was there briefly and she helped to care for me for a few days. My youngest son was gripped with fear after seeing me lying in the hospital bed barely able to breathe. He was overcome with the thought of his mother not making it through this challenge. He chose not to come back because he wanted to remember me in good health, if he lost me to this illness. I said okay God if it's my time to go, let me get my affairs/my soul in order. I gave my daughter instructions. I took care of some things I had left undone. I repented to people I had wronged. I paid back people I owed money to because I wanted to make my mistakes right.

Then I prayed, and I asked the Lord to give me more time. I was reminded of the scripture in *Isaiah 38: 1-5 KJV: In those days was Hezekiah sick unto death. And Isaiah the prophet the son of Amoz came unto him, and said unto him, Thus saith the Lord, Set thine house in order: for thou shalt die, and not live. 2 Then Hezekiah turned his face toward the wall, and prayed unto the Lord, 3 And said, Remember now, O Lord, I beseech thee, how I have walked before thee in truth and with a perfect heart, and have done that which is good in thy sight. And Hezekiah wept sore. 4 Then came the word of the Lord to Isaiah, saying, 5 Go, and say to Hezekiah, Thus saith the Lord, the God of David thy father, I have heard thy prayer, I have seen thy tears: behold, I will add unto thy days fifteen years.*

What I am saying is I was dying, I needed God's

grace and I turned my face/heart unto the Lord God and cried out unto Him. Just as Hezekiah did in the scripture. After I turned to God in prayer, the Lord answered me and gave me this scripture, *Psalm 41:1-4 KJV: Blessed is he that considereth the poor: the Lord will deliver him in time of trouble. 2 The Lord will preserve him, and keep him alive; and he shall be blessed upon the earth: and thou wilt not deliver him unto the will of his enemies. 3 The Lord will strengthen him upon the bed of languishing: thou wilt make all his bed in his sickness. 4 I said, Lord, be merciful unto me: heal my soul; for I have sinned against thee.*

Then my faith was strengthened. He reminded me just as he did Paul, my grace is sufficient. The medication had caused me to become depressed. My hallucinations caused me to think that the doctors could not remove the infection and did not want to tell me the truth. I truly thought I was dying, until the surgeon expressed that my hallucinations were side effects of the pain medication. From that point I only used the medication if I absolutely could not endure the pain. Slowly I regained my strength and the healing process began.

After 24 days of hospitalization, I was released. The surgeon told me that the right side of my upper back around my rib cage would be numb for about three months. My ability to use my right arm would also be limited. The reality of being released from the hospital with limited mobility created another set of fears. These fears turned into depression. I was a person known for helping others, it was a blow to my pride to now need help. I was excited about giving to others but having to receive was another challenge. The first thought of anyone who has faced a life-threatening illness should be a thought of gratitude and thanksgiving to God. It was a time I realized how much I needed God for literally everything and I can do nothing in and of my strength. During my recovery, my four adult children are now faced with their struggles of watching their mother recover from this illness and battling thoughts of "will my mother live through this?" My oldest daughter displayed strength for her siblings. She was there at my home everyday with her two small children. She took very good care of me; bathing, cooking, cleaning and caring for all of my needs during recovery. I couldn't help but be concerned that she might be overdoing it. My oldest son was also supportive as he could be while trying to be strong and hide his worry.

God brought us through this difficult challenge as we have experienced His healing power in operation. This life-threatening challenge has enabled us to know our God as a Healer. Through this experience as a Christian, I have learned that my faith will be tried. Through His Holy Spirit and His Holy Word, I will and can have unshakable faith. As I trust Him to guide me in my sufferings, what Satan meant for evil God used for good.

The will of my enemy is death and destruction, but the Lord Jesus Christ has overcome the sufferings of this world. In this life, we shall have tribulation, troubles and sufferings, to show us that when we accept Him (Jesus Christ) as our Savior, we too can overcome the sufferings of this world. We can allow the Holy Spirit to guide us and cause us to remain steadfast, unmovable, always abounding in the work of the Lord. Life will bring about sudden challenges, struggles, and difficulties, but through the redemptive work of the cross and putting our faith (trust) in Christ, we can have Unshakable Faith.

MEET ELDER LENORE MASON

Lenore Mason is a Native of Chicago, Illinois, an ordained Elder in the Lord's Church, a preacher, teacher of the word of God, Youth Ministry Director, prayer intercessor, mother of four children and nine grandchildren. Her areas of expertise includes mentoring women through battered crisis intervention, mentoring incarcerated women through the PLUS program (Purposeful Living Units Serve) and empowering the broken through faith. When not hard at work Lenore enjoys spending time with God in prayer and worship, reading the Bible, spending time with family and friends and cooking out.

Connect with Elder Lenore Mason:

https://www.facebook.com/lenore.walking

You're Built For This

Robin M. Adams-Massenburg

"Wait, wait, wait, Mommy, can we stay on the phone 15 more minutes? I have another story to tell you. Roz, it's going on 2:00 am. I have PT in the morning. Mommy, are you sleep?"

My house phone rang at 4:23 a.m., CPR was in progress on my healthy 22-year-old daughter with no known illnesses. I shot straight up in bed. It's my former spouse delivering the news, how could this be? I get up to start getting ready to go. To pack and move out! I'm a Soldier and I know how to do that. I've been doing that for a while now. But this mission was different because I wasn't in charge. Heck, I was losing my mind. What was coming out of my mouth was a Registered Professional Nurse with 26 years of Critical Care experience dealing with families in crisis like now. Here I was taking that same compassion with my former spouse, explaining every piece of equipment he relayed to me in the care of our child.

My husband was on the phone making travel arrangements to Indianapolis and thirty minutes later, my child was pronounced dead. Hearing a single word changed the course of my life in an instant. It was then that after 33 years in the Army, I couldn't for the life of me figure out what I was supposed to do to go on emergency leave. I called the unit, and they gave me a song and a dance. Then, I called the only person I knew who put himself out there as being genuine, the hospital Command Sergeant Major (CSM). He said he was the CSM for everyone (military, civilian, officer and enlisted). I was going to put him to the test.

"I don't know what it's like to lose a child, I'm not a mother, but I know something special is lost, all I know is how to be here for you."

I called and he answered on the first ring. I told him what was going on between sobs. He told me to go, I'll take care of everything and he did. He called every night and made sure I was ok. He talked until I felt sleepy. He still had to work in the morning. On March 18, 2016, my world was crashing. But God had already camped an Angel at my bedside and put a champion in my corner by the name of CSM Jeffrey L. Bridges. Later, I asked why he didn't sound sleepy or like I had woken him. He said God told him to get up, get dressed and he was sitting on the bed when I called. Good thing he was obedient! I'm glad he got up and did what God told him to do and was there for me. After the initial days and weeks following Rozalyn's funeral, life goes back to normal for everyone except me. My unit was unbearable.

Living a good life without any ulterior motives doesn't necessarily stop others from trying to sabotage you. This is what happened to me in my professional military career following the death of my child. I barely kept my head up or my feet moving. I looked at CSM, and the one time I ever called him by his first name, I cried when I received notice of a formal investigation against me for doing the right thing. I said, "Jeff, don't let them kick me when I'm down and can't protect myself". He said, "I won't". I left the building to seek legal counsel.

"God had the plan already worked out. His Angel was in place. He just had to prepare me."

The incident involved a Caucasian employee who called me racist and a bully and stated I tried to get her fired without proof. She was a civilian and I was in the military at the time. If I claimed anything against her, it could have been viewed as retaliation. She took this to the Commander, who launched an investigation. No one questioned the Commander's motive.

"My name may not mean anything to you, but it means something to me."

As I am going through this investigation, CSM says to me daily, "you are built for this. If you can look up, you can get up". I had to think about that and it now makes sense. People that used to talk to me began to distance themselves. Some in military leadership never offered condolences for the loss of my child. I felt as if my name and my reputation was being besmirch. I withdrew deeper and deeper into depression. One day I broke down in front of my husband. He knows the Army. He doesn't know AMEDD. I saw the fire in his eyes when he looked at me, helpless. He told me to "go home dear" and turned to walk toward the Command Suite. I called CSM and said, "Death Dealer 77" (my husband's call sign) was on his way to the Command Suite. No other words were exchanged. We hung up and CSM intercepted him. That night I received a bracelet that said, "Never Give Up." The fight was on.

I was cleared of everything! The Commander relieved, the civilian retired and life goes on. I moved from Georgia and the wounds are healing. My story doesn't end here with CSM. We adopted each other officially. Once a month, I joke about taking his CSM diploma because I haven't talked to him in two days. This is how military families do each other. He recently told me, "Big Sis you took all they threw at you, Micah 7:8 and Psalm 118 says – though I have fallen … I will rise." Show them your "Get-up Game." When I was in the storm, Jeff said I was built for it because the master made him part of the plan. I put a Post-It Note on my mirror "Now that you have my attention, God – Fix me." Part of my fix was during my last assignment in the Army. He wouldn't let me live alone as a bachelorette.

My Army family, the Justices' were my healing over coffee, laughter, TV and food. Tracy W. for a Girls Night Out and Retail Therapy. My Soror, Dena S. for Boss Ladies and Girls Getaway trips. Traci C. for inviting me into your family and getting me help when I was told the wrong thing about healthcare. Gloria B. praying for me and Pastor Ruby too, every step of the way when I needed it the most.

"My kids are my greatest treasure; I am in awe at their might."

Never underestimate the power of your children. I was so protective of my youngest daughter, making sure she was set up with all the resources and not falling apart and being her rock. We were talking about all I had gone through and she said: "Mom, God gives his toughest battles to his strongest Soldiers". God will use all of his people to deliver his message. Recently, I said people who had nothing to do with me during my storm now want to befriend me on Facebook. I don't know what's up with that and she said befriend them and give them a front-row seat to your blessings. That's powerful! I routinely Black Friday shop with my oldest son Otis. I prepare my Christmas Brunch Casserole for my youngest son Tremaine. Me and my husband James cherish our memories and make new ones. Blessed be the ties that bind our hearts together.

MEET ROBIN M. ADAMS-MASSENBURG

Robin M. Adams-Massenburg is the CEO and Founder of Robin's Nest Solutions, LLC. Robin is the creative mind in assisting fellow Veterans in navigating the Veterans Administration (VA) disabilities maze. She provides concierge veteran's claims assistance and services through Robin's Nest Solutions. Robin is a 35-year Retired Combat Veteran of the United States Army. She served 26 years as an Army Nurse Corps Officer, and the rest of her service either as an Enlisted Combat Medic or Transportation Specialist. When she's not hard at work, Robin enjoys hanging out with her family. Robin's eldest son, Otis, Jr. is an Information Technology Guru in Indianapolis and her youngest son, Tremaine, is a U.S. Marine with worldwide assignments. Other family still live in or near the "D", Detroit and it's always amazing to go home. Robin also loves to travel, shop with her friends and drive her retirement Corvette.

Connect with Robin M. Adams-Massenburg:

Website: www.robinsolves.org

Email: robinsolves@gmail.com

Release And Let Go

Evangelist Tamala Coleman

"Come to me, all you who are weary and burdened, and I will give you rest. 29 Take my yoke upon you and learn from me, for I am gentle and humble in heart, and you will find rest for your souls. 30 For my yoke is easy and my burden is light." Matthew 11:28 - 30 NIV

Life can get burdensome with the many issues that weigh us down on this journey. These things can overwhelm us. Worry, anxiety, depression, anger, guilt, shame and past hurts encumber our emotions. This list of restrictions can be endless. Burdens consume our thinking. Trials and tribulations can suck the energy out of us. I am a living witness that life's loads bring weariness and empty you spiritually, physically and emotionally. One thing we must understand is that it's not our battle. Jesus has overcome this world and we are also overcomers. So why are you trying to do it all on your own? Why have you settled for a life of stumbling under the heavy load of spiritual death? These were the questions I often asked myself as I went through a moment and time in my life that seemed like a nightmare. Yet, I had to realize that I didn't have to carry the burden alone. We can experience anxiety over things that we can't control. We must allow God to carry the burden for us. He promises that when we cast our cares upon Him, He will lighten our burdens.

Although my story has been unspoken for many years, I now have a sense of freedom, newness and restoration that God has given me. God has truly been amazing, His promises are true and I stand on every word. Now I can say that I am living my best life. Full-filling my God given talents and Gifts by allowing God to lead and direct me in making wise decisions. I choose to live happily. Sharing my testimony and my story has been enlightening. I am not ashamed anymore. I thank God for His mercy and grace.

My unspoken truth has now been told and God's plan and purpose for me continues to be revealed. God wants us to live a life of joy and newness. He wants to lead us and guide us. He also wants to show us how to get to where we need to be. Yes, I went against the grain. I suffered for a moment but my story is not uncommon. We all have our paths to travel and I surely had to endure my own. Through my journey, I can truly say that my path was leading to my destiny. Nothing worth having ever comes easy or without opposition.

Storms will come, lions will roar and our fears will be confronted. God allows the path to be difficult because He intends to refine us and prepare us for our place of promise. He is intent on extracting from us, that which our enemy would love to leverage against us. I thank God that through it all, I'm standing and I live each day with expectancy. I had to release the spiritual baggage that had me weighed down.

I remember as a young girl dreaming of being all that I can be. Growing up and having a beautiful family with a husband that treated me like a queen. Well, isn't that what many young girls dream about? I was definitely in a fantasy world back then. I saw everything with a silver lining and a bed of roses. Who would have known that I would have to live with the hand I was dealt with? In a world that was indifferent to what I wanted for myself and or imagined. I joined the church at seven-years-old and was raised in the faith.

There would be changes later in life. These changes would include turmoil, pain, heartache and a roller coaster of waves. As a youngster, all I truly wanted was to fit in and have a childhood like everyone else. Yet, there were many times I wished that I had never been born. I was the victim of bullying from elementary to high school. It was almost like I carried a sign right dab in the middle of my forehead. I always felt as though I was a target for bullying. Thank God that even through the bullying and humiliation, He bestowed His mercy. It seems so simple now, but I won't lie; I truly wanted it all to go away. I needed a temporary way out. Thank God He did not see fit for me to die. I remember going into the medicine cabinet and taking at least 15-20 pills. The outcome was only sleepiness. I continued to suffer in silence. I did not want to wear my pain on my sleeve. Through my silence my family was unable to see my suffering. *James 1:2-3 NIV, 2 Consider it pure joy, my brothers and sisters, whenever you face trials of many kinds, 3 because you know that the testing of your faith produces perseverance.*

After accepting Jesus into my life at an early age, after being in the same church all my life. God brought me back 360 to accomplish His will and plan for my life. I have a new appreciation for happiness and the joy that God gave back to me. Too many people are suffering in silence even today. There are many young people on edge. They feel as though no one cares and they have no other way out but to commit suicide. Our families, neighbors, classmates, colleagues, members at our churches and our social media friends may not look like they are struggling. However, most people do not wear their loneliness and shame openly. I was pretty good at hiding mine as well. No one knew what I was feeling on the inside. I could not talk about my loneliness. I felt no one would understand. I felt worse, worrying the people around me. I thought it was better to keep my pain to myself. I can't help but to wonder if I had done anything to deserve the treatment that I was enduring. At that time, I did not understand that "kids will be kids". Yet it was a very hurtful and trying time.

Our parents always encouraged us and made sure we were in church every Sunday. I know it was through their prayers and faith that I conquered many of the obstacles I faced. At that time I had no idea what Faith was. I am living proof that life can be meaningful, exciting and fulfilling. We should be thankful, showing gratitude for what God has done and is doing in our lives. Until you thank God for where He has brought you from, He will not take you to the place He has planned for you. Through my struggles, the devil tried to remind me of what God had not done. I had to remind him of what God has already done and will continue to do in my life. Instead of living in constant restraints I was determined to seek God for help and He has never failed me yet. I truly give all praises to God for delivering me and making a way when I could not see a way out. The Bible shares many stories of people who, like me, needed another chance and God gave it to them. I have learned to never underestimate the power of God. We serve a miraculous God. He is able to clean up any mess we can make. No one is beyond the power of God.

As a little girl to an adult woman I always felt an unusual nudge to do more. After going through and enduring so many things even up to today, I can truly say God's grace is sufficient. His grace surrounds all of us. Sometimes we see it through everyday miracles that take our breath away. I thank God everyday just for His mercy and grace alone. The grace of God can be a shelter from the darkness of this world. This is a comforting reminder for me that grace is a free gift given so generously to each of us. It was nothing but the grace of God that has brought me safe thus far.

One more detour. I married my high school

sweetheart, so I thought. My parents were so furious because they did not want me to marry him. He wasn't your typical man. He wasn't a tall man as a matter of fact he was shorter than me. He lived with his mother. He drove around with his music turned up in his car and to top it off had five kids. Naively, I was about to make a decision that would ultimately change my life. I did not think through marrying a man with multiple children when I had none. I was so naïve. I thought I was in love. I thought this was the man for me. It was lust over love or a balance that would not last. My parents did not take the engagement very well for a while. My father was determined not to walk me down the aisle. It was close to Thanksgiving and my household, as I knew it, was falling apart for almost two weeks. Thanksgiving felt like a day of sorrow; we did not have a spirit of thankfulness. It was rather dark and dreary.

In 1992, with a few family and friends, we were married. It was a church wedding at my church home. I will never forget walking down the aisle and seeing my mom crying as if she was at a funeral. I would eventually suffer the consequences of my actions and my decision to marry my now ex-husband. The first few years of my marriage, we had more sorrow than joys. I can honestly say I cried many days and nights. I was a devoted wife. I came from generations of family members who had years with their spouses. There were very few divorces in our family, including my parents, who have now been married for over 50 years. I tried with my whole being not to be a statistic and resulting in the divorce court. That was not an option for me. Yet, God had other plans and my next challenge was going to hit me like a ton of bricks.

Isaiah 40:29 ESV, "He gives power to the faint, and to him who has no might he increases strength." This scripture stuck with me through everything I endured. Living with an alcoholic whose addiction increased every day, infidelity, lies and deceit were almost a constant fight for me. With all of that, my breaking point was when I had to defend myself. As I rediscovered myself, I have learned not to conceal the pain yet talk about it, write about it and embrace it.

Over the last 17 years, this has been my mission. I don't regret the difficulties I've experienced. For they have molded and shaped me into the woman I have become today. Now I can share my story to the world so that you too can believe you are an overcomer. Release the Spiritual Baggage and let God carry the load. God Bless!

MEET EVANGELIST TAMALA COLEMAN

Tamala is a Best Seller Author and 8X Author. She is the Host of Podcast Radio show "Spiritually Speaking with Tamala Coleman" for two years. Doors continue to open for even more opportunities as Tamala moves into more Network Radio to begin in the Fall of 2020 as the owner of her own Broadcast show "Amazing Grace" which will air every Thursday Night. Tamala is an Award Winning Radio Personality of the Year for the ACHI Magazine Awards 2019. Tamala is also the owner of TC Praise Productions, LLC. It began in 2015. She produces Faith-Based Stage Plays. Tamala has been featured in the Writer's Life Magazine and Featured Cover, Voyage ATL Magazine, several radio interviews: "Fire" The Gospel Experience Radio show with Ron Jefferson, Dr. Sharon Hargro Porter on "Write the Book Now" Talk Show, YouTube Channel Authors Interview with JeQuita Zachary Johnson, "The Journey" TV Show, Straight Grown Talk TV Show, "The Jerry Royce Live show" and BlogTalk Radio. Tamala attended Ames International Biblical Ministry School in 2011, where she earned a Diploma/Certification in Biblical Studies and holds a General Ministerial License through Ames Biblical College. She has a strong track record of encouraging and inspiring everyone she meets and greets. Tamala enjoys spending time with her family, teaching and encouraging others with the word of God. Social Media Promotions:

Connect with Evangelist Tamala Coleman:

Facebook: https://www.facebook.com/tamala.coleman.1
Twitter: https://twitter.com/tamala_coleman
Instagram: iam_tamalacoleman

www.tamalacolemanbooks@yolasite.com
iHeart Podcast Website:
https://www.iheart.com/podcast/966-spiritually-speakin-29260154/

Booking Contact: Tamala Coleman
tcpraise14@gmail.com

Lost In Translation

Elder Brenda G. Williams

Yet you brought me safely from my mother's womb and led me to trust you at my mother's breast. I was thrust into your arms at my birth. You have been my God from the moment I was born. Psalm 22:9-10 (NLT)

Early Childhood~

One month and three days before my 50th birthday on Monday, August 25, 2014, this scripture from a daily prophetic devotional I received via email, came into my world/life. The light bulbs and OMGs that went off in my head! This passage of scripture gave me life. It answered and confirmed my journey in life up until that time and even to this day. I don't have a testimony of being strung out on drugs, living a promiscuous lifestyle or being homeless. My testimony will not necessarily tear a church up and have people running, jumping, hollering, speaking in tongues, or the Hammond organ and other instruments cranked all the way up. I was embarrassed and felt as if I wasn't saved enough because I didn't have such. It seemed as if these kinds of testimonies got people going and saying things like, you're anointed, you're a fireball, God got His hand on you, etc. Rarely, if ever, you heard testimonies likened to mine and I mean rarely.

I suffered badly with low self-esteem, self-worth, self-confidence and wanting to fit in with others. I didn't know why I was so different. I didn't know why I would have encounters with God. I had no context for the encounters I had with Him. I hadn't heard anyone in my family talk of such. I remember my mother asking me if I would join the church? I said yes. Mine you, we'd never had that discussion and I didn't comprehend what that meant/entailed. Envision it, Friday comes and the doors of the church are opened. I joined at the end of my first grade year, during the summer of Vacation Bible School. I left out crying and had no earthly idea as to why. I left and didn't get my hot dogs and stuff. You see on Friday, the last day of Vacation Bible School, you didn't get any juice and cookies. You got a lunch. I came home crying and my mother asked what was wrong? I told her I'd joined the church. She comforted me and let me know there was nothing wrong with that. I can remember for a period of time going to church and crying for no reason. Once when I was asked about it, I lied and said my shoes were hurting my feet. I know, shame on me. In later years, I'd come to realize God was dealing with me. I had no one to teach and instruct me on such.

I have another memory of my mother. She would read Bible stories to my sister, my brother and me. I can still see those books. I remember we would sit at her feet as she read the story and then asked us questions afterwards. Unbeknownst this time in my life would prove monumental for me.

Psalm 71:5-6 (NKJV)

5 For you are my hope, O Lord God; you are my trust from my youth. 6 By You I have been upheld from birth; you are He who took me out of my mother's womb. My praise shall be continually of you.

Junior and High School~

I would spend time nightly reading the Bible without being prompted or told to do so. Despite not comprehending what I was reading I was still motivated to do so. I remember a friend speaking boldly about God and this intrigued me. Even though I don't recall voicing it to her in retrospect, this fanned the embers of my curiosity.

The summer of my upcoming freshman year, my mother was diagnosed with breast cancer. Her treatment consisted of a mastectomy and then chemotherapy. I remember my first grade teacher and her husband would come over to have prayer and talk with her; AGLOW and the Charismatic Movement were very big. I don't recall being in the room with them. During those times when grown people were talking, children were made to leave the room. However, I guess I was close enough to hear. Likened to Joshua when God and Moses were talking. On the first day of school the summer of my sophomore year my mother passed away. I stayed with her during that hospital stay (six days) and was with her when she passed. I can remember my dad and I taking her to the hospital in Tallahassee, Fl. that Saturday morning and the conversation with the doctor. He stated she would not make it a week. I was 14-years-old. I vividly remember thinking to myself, doctor you don't know what you're talking about. I had faith that God would heal her and I prayed.

From the day she passed away until now, I never questioned God or got angry that He didn't answer my prayers. I recall my sophomore (the year of my mother's passing) and senior year having those times, once again, of reading my Bible and praying. The year 1978, due to my mother's diagnosis and subsequent passing, my role changed from one of daughter to mother/wife, figuratively. I had a younger sister and brother and can remember very vividly being told by relatives that I was their mom now; and into that role I morphed.

Friday, June 4, 1982 I graduated High School, 3rd in my class; All Glory to God! Because my life had changed, I didn't have a normal/regular childhood. I went to the club for the first time the night I graduated. It wasn't my cup of tea but that's what my classmates decided to do after graduation. My life had been put on hold and my dad thought I deserved to enjoy that day/time. I did the club thing one more time in my entire life a few months later in October for Homecoming. The next month my life would change for the best yet again.

Romans 10:9-10 (NKJV)

That if you confess with your mouth the Lord Jesus

and believe in your heart that God has raised Him from the dead You will be saved. For with the heart one believes unto righteousness and with the mouth confession is made unto salvation.

New Life~

Tuesday, November 16, 1982 I gave my life to Christ in the living room of my first grade teacher's home after Bible Study. Interesting fact, this was the same first grade teacher who had taught me the year I joined the church. Bible Study had ended and yet again I found myself having crying moments. I was crying and I didn't know what was going on. I remember my friend, my first grade teacher's daughter, took me into the bathroom and asked me if I wanted her mom to pray for me? I can't remember if I said yes or nodded my head. I remember her mom coming in and saying she's ready to be saved. Now mind you, yet again, I did not know what that meant or entailed. They bring me out into the living room and I sit in a chair. Her husband says, tell the Lord what you want. I said, I want God to save me and my family. That was it! No long drawn out speeches, just a few sincere words spoken from the depths of my heart. Those in attendance begin to celebrate and rejoice. At the time of this writing, 37 years later, I never backslide (went back into the world). Have I been perfect; No. Have I sinned; Yes. Have I made mistakes; Yes. But through it all, I really and truly love God and want to please Him with every fiber of my being.

Psalm 139:5 (ESV)

You hem me in, behind and before and lay your hand upon me.

Psalm 22:9-10 (NLT)

9 Yet you brought me safely from my mother's womb and led me to trust you at my mother's breast. 10 I was thrust into your arms at my birth. You have been my God from the moment I was born.

One day a scripture I happened to stumble upon gave me answers to my unique journey through this thing called life. My dependence upon and desperate search in the Word of God for answers and confirmation is all because I was thrust into God's arms at my birth. My passion and desire to please Him and not fail Him is all because He's been my God from the moment I was born. I am coming to realize that my parents were used as earth vessels to get me here; but I have been called by my name; I Am God's (Isaiah 43:1b)!

MEET BRENDA G. WILLIAMS

Brenda Williams is a native of Camilla, Georgia. She is a 1982 graduate of Mitchell-Baker High School and has an Associate's Degree in Elementary Education from Darton College in Albany, Georgia. She is a member of One Church, Inc. of Jacksonville; located in Jacksonville, Florida under the leadership of Apostle Leonard David and Prophet Carolyn Boston Love. There, Brenda serves on the prayer team and develops the Ministry's various newsletters. Brenda has authored (The Unique BOSS: Book Of Short Stories: The Sampler) and co-authored (50 Shades of Change), a book of prayers that addresses relevant modern day issues.

Connect with Elder Brenda G. Williams:

https://www.facebook.com/profile.php?id=100005779869754

SEEDS Familiar Bondage Over Foreign Freedom

Tomeka Wooten

My mother was 16 years of age when she gave birth to me. I grew up not knowing who my biological father was until the age of 21, after the birth of my first child. My mother and her longtime boyfriend raised me. They were blessed to have a son. He is three years younger than me. I can remember my mom's boyfriend coming to pick my mom and brother up almost every weekend. I would stand on the back porch steps of my grandparents' house crying because I wanted to go with them. I had plenty of cousins to play with, but I often felt a sense of loneliness when my mom would leave for the weekend with her boyfriend and my brother. That was the first time I can remember feeling left out, rejected and separated; therefore, I developed an even closer relationship with my grandfather. He was my only father figure at the time. We remained close until his death separated us. I can remember one incident while I was in school; I overheard a teacher refer to me as a dirty, nasty little girl to another teacher. She had invited some other girls but excluded me from coming to her house for her daughter's sleepover.

Those words "dirty little nasty girl" would affect my self-esteem for years to come. A long time ago, a well-known teacher asked me my last name while I was standing in the school lunch line. When I told her my last name, in a very negative manner, she claimed to know my whole family as if she knew me too. She made me feel so guilty about my family and who I was because of my relation to them. She treated me mean and said some hurtful things that made me feel guilty and ashamed by association. From the tender age of 7, Satan began to tell subtle lies to me, planting seeds of doubt, fear, low self-esteem, anxiety, guilt and loneliness. One night after my mom had left me with some trusted relatives, someone came into the bedroom in which I was sleeping. I remember it being very dark. Someone began to slowly pull back my covers and inappropriately touch me. I woke up screaming and they ran out of the room then out the back door.

My relatives quickly came to see what the commotion was. Although it was dark, the streets were illuminated by the street light and I saw the back of someone as they ran away. It was someone that I knew and trusted. The next morning after my mother arrived, she was told of the incident however nothing came out of it. So from that point on, I didn't see the point in telling anyone of anything else I experienced or encountered. I became somewhat anxious and withdrawn. I was so anxious at times I would suck on my index finger and twirl my hair and would pull my hair out. My hair had broken off so bad that eventually my mother had to cut it all off so that it would grow back evenly. I felt ugly and thought I looked like a boy.

There were many other times that inappropriate touching would take place by people I knew. I was made to do things that I knew were wrong, but it became normal to me. Although I knew it was wrong, a part of me felt that this was their way of showing their affection and love for me. When I was about ten years old, my mother and her boyfriend moved into a house of their own. There were many happy times but mostly, I remember, there was a lot of disagreement, arguing and physical fighting. My mother worked a lot and mainly nights, weekends and almost every holiday. I imagine work was her escape. Since I was the oldest, I was often left home to care for my siblings. When I was about 16 years old, I was criticized a lot, compared to my siblings, verbally, mentally and physically abused.

My mom's boyfriend always made sure to make me know and tell me in some way that I was not his child. He verbally blamed me for a lot regarding my mother and their troubled relationship issues. I was even told that I was the reason that he never married my mom and that he wished that I wasn't there. He would often talk down to me about my mother's side of the family whenever my mother was not around. I never told my mom how I was made to feel until I became grown. There were many other incidences in between then and now that left me feeling hurt and angry. Fast forward to 18 years old. I got into an argument and a physical altercation about my sister. I was choked, slammed on a concrete floor, had a gun drawn on me, to then have the police called on me. Although I had physical bruises, the cops did nothing. I was labeled as a disrespectful teenager. That was the day I called my mom and told her that I was leaving. I couldn't take it anymore. I went to live with my aunt for a short period of time until I got my apartment. I stopped going to church, I was raised in the church, but I was sick of rules and religion. I started indulging in drinking and smoking marijuana, taking sedatives, partying and hanging with friends. I was searching for comfort, acceptance, validation and love. I honestly didn't understand what was going on in my life. All I knew was I wasn't happy.

My brother had been imprisoned for murder. I blamed myself because I had left home. I thought that if only I had been a better sister and had not left home, he would not have gotten in any trouble. I was troubled but was trying to be strong, suppressing my feelings. I didn't realize then, but I was full of anger, bitterness and unforgiveness. After my boyfriend returned from the military, we started living together after my roommate moved out. I was financially and emotionally dependent on him. I thought he was the only one that cared about me. Everything was good between us until I got pregnant with my first son. I later found out I was not the only woman he was involved with. At that time, we could not resolve our differences, and once again, I felt rejected, abandoned and alone. I became bitter and remember thinking I was going to end up being just another statistic. I was pregnant and I felt ugly and unworthy. He eventually moved out. I refused to go back home, so I moved into another apartment that was more affordable for me.

After my son was born, I was determined to finish school, no matter how long it took. I did the best I could to provide for my son working crazy hours. We raised him the best we knew how. Our relationship was often challenged by arguments, jealousy, anger and bitterness rooted from past hurt. I longed for closure because I truly wanted to be happy and move past what I was going through. But I didn't know how. I went through clinical depression and postpartum depression. I even attempted to commit suicide once by taking pills. Although I had a child, I felt that I was unworthy of living and I thought that death would be better than the pain that I was enduring. One day my aunt took me to see a man that everyone claimed to be my father, however, my mother did not confirm those claims. I had seen him maybe twice in my life. But devastatingly, he told me I was not his daughter and that I should go and talk to my mother.

My heart was broken. I felt hopeless, again rejected. I went to my mother's house to gain clarity, but she wasn't home. As I lay in my old bedroom and just cried, I asked God why me? Shortly afterward, she came home angered to see me upset and became even angrier when she found out what my aunt had done. However, she told me the truth. She was angry at first, but she realized she had to be honest. I had learned well how to mask and suppress my feelings. But actually, I had been hurting for a long time. My mother told me the truth, and her reason for not telling me sooner. Within one week after our discussion, she told me she ran into my biological father in the grocery store. She thought he was still in California, where he had previously been living. She was shocked to see him because she had not seen him in years. She said they talked and caught up on old times. After he asked, "how I was doing?" she felt compelled to tell him about me again. She told me she felt that it was God giving her a second chance to make things right for me.

Before departing each other's presence, the opportunity presented itself when his fiancé in which he was accompanied by, decided to go to the car and wait while they caught up on old times. She proceeded to tell him once again that I was his daughter. She said his reaction was different than what she remembered years ago when she had initially told him she was pregnant. My mother didn't know how I would process things, so she gave me his phone number and address for me to call when I was ready. I found out we lived in the same apartment complex three buildings away from each other. I was excited but scared that he wouldn't like me, or he would come into my life and cause more hurt and pain adding to what I was already going through. I was very guarded. It took me two weeks to call him then finally meeting him. Today, I'm proud to say, we have a good relationship. The relationship with my father has brought about some closure and healing. The relationship that I have with my father and stepmother has greatly enriched my life. I was blessed to find out that I had known my grandparents my whole life. They were actually neighbors and good friends of my maternal grandparents. Before my grandmother died, she told me how proud she was of me and always knew it was something about me, as she watched me from her porch when I was a child. She affirmed, encouraged and most of all, she accepted me with open arms. The bond I have with my father and my brother is a bond that continues to grow stronger. We have endured some difficult times but overall I'm blessed and thankful to have them in my life.

I thought I only had one issue which was unforgiveness, but it took God to reveal to me that throughout my life, I've encountered some deep-rooted issues that spawned off from unforgiveness. I struggled with fear, shame, guilt, emotional pain, rejection, abandonment, isolation, loneliness, depression, anxiety, intimidation, infidelity, unworthiness, taken advantage of, mental, physical and sexual abuse, low self-esteem, being mistreated, talked about, lied on and lied to. I always knew I had some issues but wasn't exactly sure of what they were or how to solve them until I had an encounter with Jesus. Before then, I just suppressed a lot of my feelings until one day; I realized that I needed healing and deliverance. I wanted God to use me, and if I was to be used by God, I knew I had to be broken. Those issues broke me. I had to allow him to make me whole again because I wanted to live. The enemy was trying to destroy me, but God had a bigger plan for my life.

God dealt with the issues of my heart through my genuine submission to him. Although the foundation had been laid, I couldn't ride the coattail of my ministering mother or great grandmother anymore. I had to get to know God for myself. In 2010, at my uncle's funeral in Washington, DC, I rededicated my life to Christ and was baptized again. What the enemy meant for bad, God will turn around for the good of those that love him and called according to his plans. God overcame the world. He uses our afflictions and adversities, that through trusting in him, having faith, and through his strength, we may overcome as well. God will use us in his kingdom that we may be the voice for others that he may get all the glory! I wanted to be counted worthy and saved. We can expect to experience everything on this earth that God's own son did. We must understand that when we go through trials and tribulations, they bring forth patience, patience brings forth experience, and experience brings forth HOPE! Even in this dark and perilous world.

There is peace in having Hope that one day when he returns, that we know where we are going. I've seen and experienced the Glory of God, and I know that he's brought me a mighty long way. I've been in accidents, doctors have given me a medical diagnosis that I was told couldn't be cured, but God covered me and healed me of my afflictions. I never received an apology from some of those that hurt me in the past, but I realize that closure wasn't always necessary because The Holy Spirit interceded for me. He was and still is my comforter and protector. He has given me peace beyond my understanding, and he kept me from what could have been. Through my afflictions and adversity, I learned how to walk in a right relationship with him. I learned obedience and how to pray. He has given me knowledge, revelation, wisdom and understanding showing me the way and the truth.

My mother was kicked in her belly when she was nine months pregnant with me, but no weapons formed against me prospered. When Satan came to me as a child with seeds of suggestions, they immediately took root. That was his plan, but God! I was innocent and didn't understand what was going on, but somebody prayed for me and to God be all the Glory! If we are not careful, sin creeps in our hearts to take over, seeking to kill, steal and destroy. Sin separates us from God and is a false comforter. I despised change, was easily offended and aggravated. God started pulling back the layers of my life because he wanted to expose those roots so he can deal with them that I may be used for his glory. The Holy Spirit was teaching me how to seek His face, cast down, bind and destroy generational curses and yokes of bondage that I will be made free and whole. Before, I was used to sticking to what I knew, choosing familiarity. I chose familiar bondage over foreign freedom because it felt so good at the moment until it didn't. It was false, it wasn't lasting, nor was it real. Satan is a liar and deceiver, cunning, clever and crafty. But God is strategic, and it is only God, who is the true comfort, and because of his goodness, grace, and mercy, that he awakened my eyes to my false senses of comfort. I recognized that for me, sin never brought forth truth, healing, nor intimacy with God; therefore, these things had to be purged from me. Even though this has been ongoing for most of my life, once I allowed forgiveness of me and others to take place, the healing and deliverance started to take effect.

MEET TOMEKA WOOTEN

Tomeka Wooten is a wife, mother and author. She is the Co-Leader of Anointed Vessels (Health Care Ministry) of Living Waters Full Gospel Ministry. She attends Middle Georgia College of Theology. It is a satellite branch of North Carolina College of Theology. She is currently pursuing a Master's degree in theology in the doctoral program. Tomeka area of expertise is serving mainly in the community of healthcare for over 27 years with 16 years of actual nursing. She is a registered nurse working in the field of Oncology (Georgia Cancer Specialist affiliated with Northside Hospital of Atlanta) and also a background in Nephrology (Davita). She has certification in leadership and training. She enjoy spending time with family and friends, reading and writing, mentoring and serving.

Connect with Tomeka Wooten:

www.facebook.com/TomekaWooten

Let There Be Light!

Detrice Smith

Each time my back was up against the wall, all I've always known to do was call on Father God to get me through. God's word and faith beyond the size of a mustard seed, has always gotten me through the toughest times of my life. However, I can't say that falling on my knees to pray was the first thing I did in a crisis. I wanted to fight in the physical first, but I always remembered that God has made a way out of no way in my life. In 2002, my first husband left me and my two-year-old son after three years of marriage, but that's not my testimony.

My testimony takes place during a dark time in my life. A situation that I created. I no longer participated in church as I did growing up as a youth. However, in the midst of that dark place I knew I had to get back in right standing with God. But I didn't quite know how to get there. I was a very secretive and private person when it came to my personal life. I didn't know how to reach out for prayer and guidance. It wouldn't be until the year 2006, that I fully rededicated my life to Christ and lived according to the Word as best as I could. Now a single mother of one, for nine years, I had no choice but to put my trust in God. He was all I had to get me through the struggles of trying to raise a child while actively serving in the Army. It was not easy at all! With the daily demands of the Army and barely making enough money to pay bills. I had to make sacrifices that dug me deeper into debt. Then I found myself making choices that led to repossessions, refunded items and not being able to pay for daycare. I took a chance by opting to teach my 9-year-old how to get up, dress himself in the morning and catch the bus to and from school. God covered me through it all! I didn't want my situation to interfere in my Army career, and I needed the Army but not as much as I needed God.

Then the devil got busy in my business. Once you invite him in, he will wreak havoc on your life. Along came a man that presented himself to be someone he was not, he was very deceptive and I fell for his deception. I was not prepared for the many troubles ahead that would come with this relationship. I thought I was strong enough to withstand the trick of the enemy and could fight him off, but I fell and hard. How embarrassing it was to be serving in church, coming up as an aspiring missionary, singing in the choir, and assisting in delivering people from their demons, while being pregnant by a man who did not disclose his marital status. Just as I was coming out of my dark place from a marriage and tainted relationships, I went right back in it, but this time I dove deep. A spirit of depression took over me because I knew I let God down. I was hurt and could not forgive myself. The enemy was in my head bad, had me thinking that if I didn't eat for three days, my body would reject the baby. Oh, but can you say God protected my baby and me. I received a call on the third day, I didn't even tell anyone I was pregnant, and the words spoken to me were, "you might as well eat, it's already done!" Nothing but God. God had forgiven me, but I couldn't forgive myself, and I was messed up. I felt that "broke, busted and disgusted" feeling. I was in a deep depression. However, that same person that called me came to visit me in Newport News, VA, to break that spirit of depression off of me. That's just like God!

Despite this deliverance the enemy was still trying to destroy me through my oldest child. He had become very defiant at home and school. I had him in the right place; church. I was raising him according to the word, and he would not get right. The things I experienced with this child while also being pregnant was taking a toll on me. I somehow managed to remain steady on God's word. The more I pressed, the harder the test, but God! One of the biggest hardship was being arrested and having to plead with an intake officer to not send my child away. This experience coupled with the other things I had going on in life caused me stress, which resulted in mental health appointments and career adjustment. Through it all, I leaned on nobody but Jesus Christ. This was my breaking point and a training period to get me to the place that I needed to be in God; it was a long journey. Let there be light!

I was coming out of my dark place into a marvelous light. I finally began to see the light, I finally began to understand my purpose and who God our Father was in my life. In 2009, I was a single mother of two, active duty Army Soldier who was also a Soldier in the Army of the Lord. I stayed focused, prayed up and was running the race until I hit the finish line. Life was great! I became a founder of a church in Newport News, VA, and was appointed as the Pastor's Armor Bearer. I was a sister on fire for the Lord! I had a "For God I'll die, and for God, I'll live" spirit. Nothing could shake my faith.

In 2010, I requested to be stationed at Fort Bragg in Fayetteville, NC, to be close to my family. My family would be able to assist me with my two boys. I was very excited to be close to home, but was not ready for what was in store for me when I got there. Everything the devil could throw at me, he did. I wasn't liked by many. Traps were set in the attempt to ruin my career. People turned against me at work and church. Yes, at church, the one place I thought I would be safe from hurt. When the enemy plants a seed it could cause leaders, the church and even Pastors to question who you are in the faith. However, God had a better plan to get me away from all the confusion and turmoil in my life.

In 2014 my little family and I went to Korea, where my life of ministry began. For about a year, just a season, I started a Sunday bible-teaching ministry. Believe it or not, I had a few faithful members. It was just the right amount for me. The people who needed to be there was there. God will provide a light in the dark places of your life, just like He did for the Israelite's. No matter the situation or how hard life is sometimes, just put all your trust in God, and He'll get you through it! I'm a living testimony, time and time again when I found myself in a dark place; all I had to do was look up towards the light, Jesus!

MEET DETRICE SMITH

Detrice Smith was born in Victorville, CA. on 4 January 1975. Her areas of expertise include Catering, Event Planning and Music and Entertainment Management. When not hard at work, Detrice enjoys designing T-shirts, cooking and traveling. She has an Associate's Degree in General Studies and a Medical Assistant Diploma. She is currently enrolled in Colorado Technical University pursuing a Bachelor's of Science Degree in Logistics and Supply Chain Management.

Connect with Detrice Smith:

Facebook: www.facebook.com/DetriceSmith

Recovery From The Unknown Trauma

Pastor Sharon Burrell

It was early morning when I awoke with beads of sweat on my forehead and a feeling of anxiousness. I sat up in bed wondering what was causing my heart to palpitate so frantically. Did I have a dream or was it a nightmare? I sat there for a few hours, racking my brain, trying to locate the perpetrator of my fear. My back straightened as it dawned on me this was something from my past. Yes! It was incidents of my past that I so carefully tucked away deep in my subconscious. I did not have a bad dream. It was not a nightmare but the features of my subconscious. These were the realities of rape, molestations and sexual assaults that took center stage of my mind. As I sat still in bed I thought I was reliving the sexual intrusions, which started from the young age of four. This nightmare went on until age ten. Then a year of nothing; thinking to myself, oh God it has finally ended. Only to discover that freedom was short-lived. At the age of eleven, it started again and at the age of fifteen, I brought it to a complete end.

It was 1994 and I was attending Housatonic Community Technical College. I was going to further my education in Human Services as I wanted to become a Pastoral Counselor or Social Worker. I was given an assignment in my Communication class. The assignment was to write about something special from my childhood, a person, place or thing. I was indecisive on whether to write about my pet dog named Bruno or my gold and brown teddy bear. I pondered with the idea that I would write about my loving pet Bruno. Before going to bed I jotted down various ideas on what to write regarding my dog. I was nervous about writing my story because though I am outgoing and friendly. I am also shy. As the deadline for the paper drew near I started to write about my dog. I viewed Bruno as being part of me as he was my constant companion. When he died, I wanted to die too. I was only nine when I lost him. I cried for many days and could not be consoled, so my aunt, whom I lived with at the time, bought me another dog that I also grew to love. It was two days before my paper was due so I sat down and racked my brain on how to put the story together. I jotted down the names of everyone that was in the family and the different role they played in my life. I completed my assignment the night before my class. I went to bed oblivious of past trauma tucked so neatly away in my subconscious.

I awoke between the hours of 3 a.m. and 4 a.m. I was breathing heavily with tears running down my face and overwhelming emotion of anxiety. It went on for a few hours as I sat looking into the darkness. I sat there wondering what was causing my heart to palpitate so rapidly. Not sure why this was happening because reality has not set in yet. I turned over and tried to go back to bed because I was too weak to get up and go to work. I did manage to fall asleep and when I awoke I called my work place and called out. As I laid in bed reality washed over me like a surfer who was suddenly slammed into a big wave. Once again, I started crying, this time I cried in silence because I did not want my husband or my children to see the pain or anguish I was experiencing. I told my husband I was not feeling well and was staying home from work. I explained to him that what I was going through would soon pass and I would be able to go to my classes. Everyone had left. As I lay down and thought about the rush of memories, which now, filled my mind and invaded my heart. Different emotions washed over me as I went from feeling deflated, depress, lonely, anxious, unloved and finally angry. I was so angry that I went and changed different parts of my assignment.

The changes I made reflected some of the pain I felt that would not and could not stop. The pain could not stop because it was harsh and raw. Though the memory was real, the role of pretense that I played before my family was also real. You see, I had first hand practice on keeping the pain and reality of the trauma under a smile and a laugh. I had to practice it for many years because everything I went through back then was given many faces. Of the many faces, the one that became my favorite was the mask. With the mask, I smiled, laughed and showed joy. All my emotions were bottled up on the inside and were untouchable. I cried for most of the day because my mask was leaking from all the cracks that happened within that moment. I pulled myself together because my children would be coming home from school soon. I cleaned the house, prepared dinner and took my shower, as I would be leaving for classes momentarily. Everyone was in place except my oldest boy and my husband would be home a little later. My son arrived just as I was about to leave and this was a joy to my heart because he changed after my marriage.

I left for school and my first class was my communication class. I arrived still feeling anxious, but I was not going to put another crack in it, so I stayed focused. As the class progressed and each person went up to read their story, I became nervous as my time to read was coming up. I got up and started my story about my pet dog Bruno, but just like that, everything changed. I had to tell my truth regarding my experience this morning, which led up to right now. I was not sure how my classmates or my professor would react, but I had to let it out. Half of my mask crumbled and shattered right before everyone's eyes. I would have felt terrible and deflated, but instead, a sigh of relief left my lips. Everyone started apologizing for enduring my traumatic experience. I never felt so much compassion from people I did not know, but it helped relieve my anxiety at the moment. The class finished on a positive note as my professor explained he has seen and heard many things, but he appreciated this sigh of relief in its moment. My next class was Human Service and my professor was a Psychologist. I believed this was the LORD'S doing because my communication class let out early, and when I arrived at the Human Service class, the professor was already there; he was early. I approached my professor and told him what I had experienced and still experiencing regarding the unfolding flood of memories I had locked away for many years. He took me through a short counseling process that made me feel relaxed enough to finish all my classes.

I got home with what was left of my mask intact. I laughed and played with my children and helped them as best that I could at that moment. My children were my joy and my strength before giving my life to JESUS CHRIST. So when I arrived home that night, I draw strength from my family. I went through my daily routine without my family, knowing how much I was hurting. My family never knew the extent of my pain and blame I put on myself for being stupid and simple. I did tell my family what I experienced and my children were angry and showed understanding beyond comprehension. As the cracks in my mask continued leaking, I started praying for myself as this was something I rarely do. I usually pray for everyone else, the sick, children and the world. I started quoting different Psalms from the bible to prevent an explosion of self. I read the word of God at every opportunity because I have to keep my sanity for my children's sake. Away from my God, my children were and are my life. I remained intact with the help of God until I relocated to Savannah, Georgia. Ten years I leaked and spilled in silence. But the other half of the mask started slipping and I had to leave everyone and everything behind. So I relocated to regain control of myself and my life before I lost me. The hurt was so deep and severe I needed space. I needed a new city, town or state to find a new way of functioning.

With the Lord's permission, I moved to Savannah. I stayed praying, fasting and visiting churches. I started to become the real me as I have been a people-pleaser during my non-existing self. I was living for everyone else, but now I do me and I discover that people did not like the out-spoken, very direct me. Hey! But I loved being me. I started facing my past head-on by quoting scriptures of God's promises and basking in His love for me. Though I had four children, I never really loved any of their fathers. I only had intimate relations because I believed that's the only thing men wanted. I never gave my heart away and as soon as I got pregnant, I left the relationships. The person I had the longest relationship with was my last child's father. He chased me for five years and while together, he treated me like a queen and he was totally in love with me. The others liked me but not sure if any love was there. Away from my first relationship, the others were fun and enjoyable. As I started evaluating my life, I realized I didn't know me. I knew the foods I liked, I knew I liked watching television and going to the movies. I did not realize I had preferences in what I watched on TV. I did not know I had a dress style, fetish for shoes, shades, pens, towels and perfumes. Having constant fellowship with Jesus caused me to tolerate myself and gain confidence in myself.

I believed the Lord when He says I am with you, I will never leave nor will I forsake you. Jesus let me know that He loves me. I spoke Psalms 91, 23, 27, 42, 46 and 51 if I felt I did something out of the will of God. I always pray and give the Lord His words back. *Romans 12:1-2. I beseech you therefore, brethren, by the mercies of God, that you present your bodies a living sacrifice, holy, acceptable to God, which is your reasonable service. And be not conformed to this world, but be transformed by the renewing of your mind, that you may prove what is that good, and acceptable and perfect will of God.* I would recite that faith without works is dead and that without faith it is impossible to please God. I would ask God daily *Psalm 51:10 - Create in me a clean heart, O God; and renew a right spirit within me.* My desire was to please God in all that I do. I look at Jesus as my father, my brother and my husband. I did not know the love of a father or mother. So my desire was to make the person who was and is keeping me alive (Jesus) happy with me. I looked to Jesus for everything and believed Him for my deliverance and healing of the past trauma. Eventually, I found myself talking freely about the molestation, rape and sexual assaults. One day I realized I went from hurting and crying to thanking God for what I went through. I found myself saying to everyone that I spoke with; I know Jesus was with me in my ordeal because I never got pregnant or contracted any sexually transmitted diseases. I had complete faith in Jesus that He would bring me out of the stupor I felt.

My attitude and emotions changed though I am still a little harsh and aggressive in all that I do. I have a true love for all humankind. I never believed anyone loved me even though they said so. But today, because of my faith in Jesus, because I am truly delivered, I can say that I now bask in the love and favor of others. I am a different person because I have unshakable faith in Jesus Christ, my Lord. He was and is truly a way maker, a provider and very present help in the time of trouble. He is the lifter of my soul, my joy river and my peace giver. Without Him, I would be nothing. He is the reason I am living and I praise Him every day for His mercy in my life. Thank you, Lord, for loving me.

MEET PASTOR SHARON BURRELL

Sharon Burrell is the supporting Pastor at Grace and Abundance Fellowship Ministries. As a motivational speaker she empowers others through her ministry. She's also a former Director of Group Homes with an expertise in Mental Health counseling. When not hard at work Sharon enjoys seeking God as well as researching various subjects pertaining to life.

Connect with Pastor Sharon Burrell:

https://www.facebook.com/sharon.burrell.3958

The Guiding Light

Cassandra Brown Moody

I was raised in the small town of Fort Valley, GA. The oldest of four children and the only girl. Even though we didn't go to church every Sunday, God was the head of our lives. We had little growing up but had a love of our family and Christ. The bible says in *Hebrews 11:1, KVJ "Now faith is the substance of things hoped for, the evidence of things not seen."* As a child growing up I was always obedient, but I wanted more out of life. I questioned God asking why I can't have or live a high life. People would always tell me you will be somebody because you are smart and very creative. I didn't see what others saw in me. I felt something was missing.

I ran away from home at seventeen. Once I left home I was fearful of becoming a statistic, pregnant, on welfare, and without an education. I proved the naysayers wrong. I earned three degrees and later secured a great job. Despite my best effort, I wasn't fulfilled and didn't feel whole. I realized I needed to depend on God more than ever. It was then I discovered I didn't have a true relationship with Christ.

In 2009, I woke up in the hospital after having preeclampsia and seizures related to the birth of my newborn baby. I was unconscious for three days. An older lady in the hospital kept asking me about my husband. I kept telling her I didn't know and to leave me alone. She stayed by my side and wouldn't let me go to sleep. After gaining consciousness, I asked the staff about the nurse and no one knew who I was talking about. I kept quiet because I didn't want anyone to think I was crazy. At that moment I knew she had to be my guardian angel. I thought about the struggles I had gone through and needed to share. All I could hear was, *Jeremiah 29:11, KJV "For I know the thoughts that I think toward you, saith the Lord, thoughts of peace, and not of evil, to give you an expected end".* At this time, I was going through a divorce, had given birth to my fourth child and working paycheck to paycheck.

After leaving the hospital, I found a church home and got saved. It was an amazing feeling. I was now beginning to feel whole as I drew closer to Christ and nothing could change it. There was a complete shift. Just as Christ has given to us, I shared my gifts with others. My mindset shifted from wanting to be served to serving our communities.

I started my own business and walked away from my corporate job after fifteen years. My goal is to help create wealth and mentor those wanting financial freedom. After hitting six figures in my financial business, I want others to learn about success and ownership. Along this amazing journey of faith, I found my soulmate. He loves, encourages and supports me and I couldn't ask for a better mate. The biggest accomplishment is time, freedom and time spent with my children. You must cherish time because it is something you can't get back. *Mathew 6:33, KJV "But seek ye first the kingdom of God, and his righteousness; and all these things shall be added unto you."*

God divinely restored my life by rescuing me from myself. For those of you who are trying to find your way, look to God and trust his every word.

MEET CASSANDRA BROWN MOODY

Cassandra Brown Moody is a Wife, Mom & Mogul! In her spare time she enjoys spending time with her husband, four children and grandchild. She loves to read, travel and meet great people. In 2010, Cassandra stepped out on faith and started her own business. She believes financial education literacy is so important. She started to travel, educate, empower and share her experiences with individuals, schools, churches and the community. Cassandra loves connecting with people from all walks of life and is very passionate about helping others WIN. Her motto is "What You Put Out Is What You Attract." Start each day with a positive thought and a grateful heart. Cassandra Moody is the CEO of Brown's Precise Consulting.

Connect with Cassandra Brown Moody:

Website: www.brownspreciseconsulting.com

Contact: 478-923-5022

The Prodigal Daughter

Jenise Albritton

Dear Lord, forgive me. I have fallen to your mercy. I am weary and ask for your grace and mercy to let me experience your Glory once again! Thank you for keeping me. You left the other 99 just for me. I want to come back home to you, Lord! Cleanse me, oh Lord, and renew my spirit. Make me whole again, better than new. I am your daughter, and you are my Father. Thank you God, I love you; Amen!

When we are born, we come from the womb to see our assigned earthly mother and father. After spending time in heaven with God, long before our souls are assigned to be born to our earthly bodies, we've experienced the love of God and have come to know his greatness. When we are born, we have no choice about the family we are born into. We could be assigned to the most God-fearing, loving, caring and beautiful family on earth. Or we could be assigned to the most dysfunctional, unkind and hate-filled family. Then there is always the in between, the grey area which provides you with the best or worst of both worlds. As we grow older we try to understand the family we are born into. We either embrace our family or distance ourselves from them. If we ever experience the love of God, it will always call us back home. Just a taste of his love, is more than enough to forgive us, no matter what we do.

My parents divorced when I was three years old. The images play in my head of when and where everything changed for me. From being over my grandma's house, my dad left with a lady, and my mom went next door. I'm crying for my mom hysterically, a cranky three-year-old ready to go home. My dad comes back looking for my mom; he takes me home, and gives me the whooping of my life with a bath brush. I went to bed, unable to sleep. Later that evening I hear arguing and I jump up to see a horrible vision of my dad over my mom with knives in his back pocket. Neighbors come in and just like that all is forgotten. This was the beginning of being displaced and the seeds of running away had been planted. For most of my childhood I remember being left with my grandma and my aunt after school and over the weekends. If I was home, I would be there alone. When my mom and I were home together, it would be turmoil. So much bitterness and anger filled the house. I was constantly picked on everywhere I went, and experiencing the same torment at home did not help.

The only escape was church. One of my greatest escapes was a summer in New York with one of my aunts. I got saved at age 7. I experienced love, peace and joy. I saw and felt how beautiful life could be. I would hold onto those feelings and visions, carrying them with me when I went back home.

Growing up in the projects was tough. If it seemed like you were doing just a little better you were picked on and frowned upon. The same also happened if it seemed like you were doing worse. There just wasn't any escape. As I matured, my body began to develop, and I looked for the love I felt I was missing from my parents. My dad didn't come around much except when my mom called to complain and give him negative reports about me. Anything she thought she could say about me to get him to come around and possibly get his attention. I began to use crush pills. I would keep them in a bottle, in a corner under my dresser. I'd hang out at night and wear short dresses and revealing clothing to get attention. It was what my so-called friends were doing. My mom wasn't paying me any mind, and she bought the clothes. I was running the streets late at night with the other girls from school that also lived in the PJ's with me. I dealt with guys that had no good intentions for my life. They didn't even have good intentions, dreams or ambitions for their own lives. However, I was still with them, still looking for something they couldn't give. Something they'd probably never been given and that was love, real love.

At the age of 13, I lost my virginity. My mental state was unclear; I was lost and searching for myself amidst the mess. I found myself back at the altar, praying to God for help. The word "no" gave me a permanent scar on my left leg as the one who took that virginity, hurled it at me. I found myself running down the street in tears telling my mom I fell. I did, I fell to my knees in prayer. God always tugged on my heart since the day I got saved. In spite of that, I couldn't see how much God loved me. The love I was looking for, I had it all along; in Him! I was running from everything and everyone. Running to the Ibuprofen mixed with Advil and God knows whatever else I could find to zone out!

Another great escape was my room and video games. I also loved getting good grades in all my classes. The band was another outlet. I loved music. I always credit the band for saving my life. As I transitioned to high school, I watched those same girls I used to run with continue to run behind boys in men's bodies. Some of them became pregnant. By that time I was heavily involved in church, singing in the choir and a member of the youth group. I expressed to my dad in a letter that I needed him to be there for me. My dad had always been my motivation to do my best. Whenever I made mistakes, he never judged me. I thank God for the band and seeing different places while traveling. I always say the band saved my life. It kept me from being a statistic. I've been running all my life. Looking and searching for the things I couldn't see, but have been inside of me all the time. God has never left my side. From dancing in the strip club, making ends meet, dating so-called dope boys, felons and trusting crooked people and so much more. God has kept me in his grace. Through joblessness, homelessness, being broke, down and out and thoughts of suicide, he always continued to tug on my heart calling me back to the church. He always called me back to my earthly father and reminded me that someone was rooting for me to make it. That everyone wasn't out to do me wrong and leave me hanging.

Now as a woman in my 30's, I admit, I still struggle with believing if people are rooting for me to make it or rooting for my downfall. My dad has always been that one consistent person in my life. When family turns their noses up at me, fails to support me, smiles but offers no help; I still have my dad. I will always have him as a means of support even if nobody else gets me. My dad and I have had our differences but I always come back home because, like my heavenly father, he always welcomes me with open arms. No judgment, no condemning, no shaming, just love, encouragement and motivation. He tells me how much he believes in me and encourages me to keep pressing towards my dreams! Comparing me to my Grandma Dora. She traveled the world, seeing many great sites, meeting great people and living life the way it should be lived. She touched the lives of many. People get lost in the world trying to live up to other people's expectations. Expectations that are not even met by the people they look up to. We lose ourselves trying to find ourselves in the world. I thank God for free will. Choosing him allows me to exercise that right, that's how you know it's from the heart and that's how God knows you really want him in your life. No matter what though, he always wants you in his life because you are his child.

The Bible speaks on the Prodigal Son, but what about the prodigal daughters in the world? Often the women are left to fend for themselves at an early age. They find themselves taking care of siblings because of absent parents. Some are on the street corners trying to make ends meet to provide for themselves and others. Maybe they are looking for love they didn't get growing up. Love they never saw but only heard of. Not knowing God's love has been with them the whole time. Maybe nobody told them or showed them those scriptures.

As the child bearers, women experience many hurts, pain, emptiness and lonely feelings that come from mindless sessions of intercourse. They in turn share these feelings with the children that they bear, not becoming wives but only baby mama's. The streets didn't tell them and life has drained them of any hope of finding the one God made for them. If they knew the story of Boaz they would know there is someone out there for them. Understanding that God is the ultimate man in their life. That he wants the absolute best for his daughters, even more than she wants for herself. God is her first love. Once she gets to know his love, it will always call her home and God will always welcome her back.

God: Do you not know who I am?

Daughter: No, but I feel like I should know who you are. Tell me…

God: I am your father.

Daughter: My father is dead! He left me a long time ago.

God: I am your Heavenly Father. The one who created you. I created you in my image.

Daughter: Why have I never heard of you? Do you know what I've been through?

God: Yes, I do. I've been with you the whole way through. In those darkest hours is when I carried you.

Daughter: Why did you let me go through the things I've been through?

God: I give free will. I send those to preach the gospel through the earth. I never gave you more than I knew you could bear.

Daughter: I was lonely. I was hurt. Where were you?!

God: Holding you. Carrying you. Walking beside you. I am here love. Take my hand. Will you?

Daughter: Yes…

MEET JENISE ALBRITTON

Terika Jenise Albritton (JENISE or JEN LO) is a Life Changer at Total Life Changes. Her area of expertise is helping people around the world to get healthy, lose weight, feel great and earn income while doing it. She is also a motivational speaker who shares nuggets and tips on how to overcome life's obstacles by looking at life with a positive, open, mindset. As well as a model, actress, event host, wig maker and more!

Connect with Jenise Albritton:

Facebook Pages: Jen Lo Assassin and Second Chance 21013

Instagram: @JenLoAssassin @SecondChance_21013

Twitter: @JenLoAssassin

About the Author

Evangelist Tomika Prouty is the Owner/CEO of House of Stone by CoCo, LLC. It was launched as an online company in August 2014. Her company initially started with the sale of t-shirts that display positive Christian messages such as “Turn’t Up 4 JESUS” and rapidly expanded into an international market with customers in France, Germany and Kuwait (as well as the U.S.). She is a Celebrity Jewelry Designer Visionary; uniquely designed, handcrafted, one-of-a-kind jewelry creations, which exudes elegance, grace & sophistication as well as pieces for “everyday wear”. She dedicated twenty-two years of life serving (Retired/Combat Veteran) in the United States Army. She would not be the woman she is today and where she is in life without her Lord and Savior Jesus Christ. She is truly passionate about her relationship with Him and why she penned her first Memoir, A Soldier’s Story: Strength Despite Adversity (March 2018). She discussed the hard truth about war and how she overcame many obstacles that were meant to destroy her. But God! She also co-authored Daughters of Triumph (November 2018) with twenty amazing women. She is the Visionary of Unshakable Faith, Twenty Testimonies by Men & Women of Great Faith! She is happy to announce that this is the first of many books published under House of Stone Publishing. **Coming soon, a talk show with Tomika Prouty**! She currently reside in Bonaire,

Georgia and like most business professionals; she has her hands full as a wife, mother, visionary, speaker, author, writer, blogger, and Co-Founder of Truth Revealed Global Ministries (September 2016). She is currently pursuing a graduate degree in theology. Truth Revealed (Outreach/Street Ministry) motto is "meeting people where they are". They believe in going out into the community meeting the needs of the people; serving others not being served.

You can connect with Evangelist Tomika Prouty on:

www.tomikaprouty.com

www.facebook.com/HouseOfStoneByCoCo

www.instagram.com/houseofstonebycoco

houseofstonebycoco@gmail.com

www.ingramcontent.com/pod-product-compliance
Lightning Source LLC
Chambersburg PA
CBHW071933090426
42811CB00042B/2425/J